MASTERING YOUR BUSINESS DISSERTATION

The ability to write to a high standard is a key skill that is often over-looked in the business world. This short book from an international, best-selling author is a practical guide to conceiving, researching and writing a business or management dissertation.

Robert Lomas offers an inspirational treatise that will awaken the quest for knowledge among his readership. This book helps business students to frame their research questions in the best way to achieve their research aims and to write in a clear and top-scoring way. Topics covered include collecting and measuring data, using business statistics, planning research projects and the real mechanics of writing a dissertation.

Masters students across business and management will benefit enormously from reading this book, not just through adding serious value to their dissertations, but also through improving their writing skills for the rest of their business careers.

Robert Lomas is Lecturer in Technological Management at the University of Bradford, UK. He is the course leader for the MBA Business Research Module and has also written best-selling books, including *The Hiram Key*, *Turning the Hiram Key* and *The Invisible College*.

MASTERING YOUR BUSINESS DISSERTATION

How to conceive, research, and write a good business dissertation

Robert Lomas

Routledge
Taylor & Francis Group

LONDON AND NEW YORK

First published 2011
by Routledge
2 Park Square, Milton Park, Abingdon, Oxon OX14 4RN

Simultaneously published in the USA and Canada
by Routledge
270 Madison Avenue, New York, NY 10016

Routledge is an imprint of the Taylor & Francis Group, an Informa business

Typeset in Aldus and Gill Sans by
Florence Production Ltd, Stoodleigh, Devon
Printed and bound by
the MPG Books Group in the UK

British Library Cataloguing in Publication Data
A catalogue record for this book is available from the British Library

Library of Congress Cataloguing in Publication Data
Lomas, Robert, 1947–
    Mastering your business dissertation : conceiving, research, and
    writing for a masters degree / Robert Lomas.
      p. cm.
    1. Business—Research. 2. Dissertations, Academic.
    3. Business writing. I. Title.
    HD30.4.L66 2010
    650.072—dc22   2010021064

ISBN: 978–0–415–59678–7 (hbk)
ISBN: 978–0–415–59679–4 (pbk)
ISBN: 978–0–203–09314–6 (ebk)

To Mark Booth,
publisher, editor, writer and businessman
– the man who taught me how to write

CONTENTS

LIST OF FIGURES

LIST OF TABLES

FOREWORD

I met Robert Lomas in 2000 when I made an offer to publish *The Hiram Key*, his first book, co-written with Christopher Knight.

The first thing that impressed me about him was his courage. Here was an academic and a Freemason saying things that were bound to outrage many in both communities.

The second thing was his determination to be clear. *The Hiram Key* is packed with new research and original ideas emerging from that research. The sheer volume of information the reader is asked to absorb threatens to be overwhelming, and many of the ideas are new and quite hard. In the hands of a lesser writer, the effect on the reader might have been like trying to walk head-on into a snowstorm.

But where some writers might have been tempted to hide behind deliberate obfuscation, or to enjoy mystifying the reader, Robert was evidently determined to lay out these ideas and these facts in as plain a way as possible.

He had also taken care to organize his ideas in a way that shows a progression. There was an unfolding of understanding that pulled the reader through some four hundred pages at a spanking pace. By the end of the book the reader had taken in much that was new, hard, even abstruse – without being conscious of having made an effort. This is why *The Hiram Key*, as well as being a best-seller all around the world upon publication, continues to sell and sell.

The Hiram Key has an historical narrative, but that is not true of all Robert's books. Even where there isn't an obvious chronological narrative around which to weave the development of his ideas, Robert is a master of the art of making people want to know What happens next? This art lies in asking questions, posing problems to be solved, pointing out inconsistencies in the commonly accepted view, and drawing attention to the fact that there is treasure to be discovered.

The aim is always to bring the reader to a clear understanding, and the digital revolution makes clarity all the more important. When I started in publishing some twenty years ago, I might have received a handful of submissions per week through the post. Perhaps a couple of internal memos would flutter down into my in-tray per week. 'Those can simmer for a while,' I used to think, as I went back to staring out of the window and making grand plans.

These days I receive anywhere between a hundred and two hundred emails per day, many of them business propositions and most of them expecting a quick response. I receive about thirty submissions per week. God does not send enough hours to read all this stuff. The propositions that have the boldness and clarity that Robert Lomas teaches in this book are the ones I make the time to read. I suspect the same is true in other businesses.

Whether we are talking about ideas for best-selling books or any other business proposition, there is, I believe, a magic in clarity. Clarity helps ideas become real.

The British philosophical tradition lays much more emphasis on clarity than, say, the French or the German. Is this because in Britain philosophy has been more closely tied to the growth of scientific thinking? As a scientist Robert probably knows the answer.

Why is it that if a scientific theory is clear and simple, even elegantly so, it is more likely to be right?

Is the cosmos – no less than Robert Lomas – trying to tell us something?

ACKNOWLEDGMENTS

As a young physicist, I was fortunate to have Prof. Michael Hampshire of Salford University as my PhD supervisor. Mike taught me how important it was to be curious and to ask the right sort of questions, and I am grateful to him for providing me with this useful skill, which I have cultivated and now try to pass on to my own students.

I would also like to express my gratitude to Mark Booth for teaching me how to write. Mark is one of the publishing industry's most successful players. After university he started out as a bookseller with Waterstones, where Tim Waterstone spotted his talent and invited him to devise a new imprint. Going from total publishing inexperience to running his own list in a matter of months, he was an immediate success as a commissioning editor. Over the last twenty years or so he has produced two or three top-ten best-sellers every year and has invented at least two new publishing genres: the SAS thrillers of Chris Ryan and the 'chav-lit' novels of Katie Price. And Mark has an uncanny nose for unlikely bestsellers – a skill he puts down to being a good listener. He's published Banksy, the graffiti artist; Valentino Rossi, the motorcycle champion; Marti Caine, the comedian; and Boyzone pop-singer Stephen Gately's posthumous novel *Tree of Seasons*.

He has also published me. When I first ventured beyond academic textbook-writing into the hard commercial world of trade books, Mark Booth was commissioning editor at Century (a Random House imprint). He took the rather muddled manuscript of *The Hiram Key*, which I had written with my friend Chris Knight, and showed me how to improve it, focus its message and cut the waffle out. It was an immediate best-seller and remains an evergreen. Since then I have written many other successful books, and still enjoy working with Mark at his new imprint.

From our first meeting Mark has encouraged me to ask the sort of interesting questions Mike Hampshire would have approved of, to provide good evidence to support my answers and to write a good story telling how it happened. I want to thank Mark for all he has taught me about the art of writing. It is his message about the joy of asking a good question and the pleasure of composing a clear answer which inspired me to pass his ideas about writing on to the students whose dissertations I was supervising. The result was a whole string of distinctions.

This was spotted by Prof. James Powell of Salford University, then external examiner for the Bradford MBA in Engineering Management. James found my students' dissertations amazingly readable and consistent in standard, and he asked me what I was doing. When I explained, he encouraged me to share these good writing concepts more widely, both with my colleagues and with my students. I am grateful to James for his friendship, our fascinating discussions and his academic encouragement to tackle an issue often neglected in dissertation supervision: teaching your students to write well and to think clearly about what they should write.

I would also like to thank Terry Clague of Routledge, who dropped in for a chat just when I was developing the material for a course at Bradford School of Management. He looked at my lecture outlines and course objectives and suggested the concept would make a textbook rather different from most existing ones. He encouraged and guided me to write this, my first textbook since 1985, and I have enjoyed doing it.

Finally I am grateful to Dr Roger Beach and Prof. Kevin Barber – my academic colleagues at Bradford School of Management, who incited me to be ambitious in setting high targets for my MBA students, and to John Wheelwright, my long-time copy-editor and a stalwart guardian of the art of clear writing, for providing a second pair of eyes and a sense of clarity. But most of all I want to thank my students, who worked so hard, and contributed so many useful thoughts, during the 2009 Business Research Course where I formally piloted the ideas set out here.

ROBERT LOMAS

Bradford University School of Management, 2010

THE PURPOSE OF THIS BOOK

The chapters of this book were written as a series of weekly lectures for a part-time MBA evening course in Research Methods for students at Bradford University School of Management.

Its aim was to give an oversight of all the skills students would need in order to produce an acceptable dissertation in Business or Management, and also to motivate them to approach the dissertation as a chance to learn about the subject, about their roles in their company and about themselves. In any postgraduate business degree it is the dissertation that provides the greatest opportunity for learning and bringing together all the subjects studied. However, students often see dissertation-writing as a necessary evil – something they try to dash off as quickly as possible in order to finish the course and get a pass. I set out to try to transform this view, so that my students would look forward to the chance to research a topic that fascinated them and would help them establish themselves in a future career.

My method of delivery was first to deliver the material here contained in a chapter as a lecture, then divide the students into groups. (I took care to categorize all students according to two basic viewpoints about research, which I called Platonist and Aristotelian. I then allocated them into groups that contained representatives of each viewpoint, to ensure balance in discussion.)

After the lecture, lasting about an hour, we would break for dinner, then return refreshed to spend the next hour debating the topics put forward in the lecture. The students were split into groups of five or six, and each group went to a separate syndicate room to discuss a set topic relating to the lecture material (these topics are included at the end of each chapter of this book). I circulated among the groups asking questions, provoking thought and generally stirring up each group to really question what it meant to research and write a dissertation.

Finally the groups would reassemble in the lecture theatre, and each would summarize its views on the topic before I facilitated a final plenary discussion to reinforce the findings. The whole process took about three hours.

After the initial group session I asked them to think about the motives of the main stakeholders and set them an individual task of writing to a deadline. The topic is shown at the end of Chapter 1, and the report they produced formed the beginning of the Learning Log I encouraged each student to keep to create a personal record of each of the discussions. The aim of the Learning Log was to capture, not only what they were learning but also how they felt about being challenged, and how hard it sometimes was to face up to difficult issues of motivation and time-management.

The first written assignment served three purposes.

- It showed it was quite possible to write text of a set length, on a set topic, to be delivered to a tight deadline. In other words, you don't need to wait for inspiration to strike. You can sit down in front of a blank page and write to order. The writing may not be perfect, or even as good as you would like, but, once you have something written, it becomes possible to edit and improve what you have, and your thoughts become much clearer.
- It forced each individual to write down their own motives, and the motives they ascribed to the other key stakeholders in the dissertation.
- It provided basic material, to be used in later group discussions to conceive a good research question – one that could satisfy all the criteria for planning a dissertation that would be interesting to all stakeholders, that it would be possible to answer within the assigned word count and time limit, and that would get a good mark when submitted for examination.

Over the following weeks the groups explored all the key issues in the process of dissertation creation. And they built up Learning

Logs that were relevant to the problems they would address when working on their own dissertations.

The final learning took place during the final exam, which was an open book – meaning students could take any material they wished into the exam. During the two hours of the exam the students were asked to use their Learning Logs to produce a dissertation proposal and a plan of implementation.

When the course began all the students were nervous and fearful about trying to write what seemed to them a long document on a boring topic. When it ended I had a group of keen researchers eager to seize the chance to study and learn about something that interested them and offered them the prospect of becoming an expert on a topic they could use to advance their career.

HOW TO USE THIS BOOK

If this book is used as a textbook, then all the tasks are set. If you are using this book as an individual, I suggest that, after reading each chapter and before reading on, you take time to write out your own answers to the discussion topics in a Learning Log. By thinking, and writing, about each topic before reading further you will find you have prepared your mind to learn more from the next chapter/lecture.

Writing a business dissertation can be a joyful learning experience. The aim of this little book is to show how to approach this happy state.

1

UNDERSTANDING BUSINESS RESEARCH

WHY RESEARCH?

R ESEARCH IS A STRANGE WORD. At first meeting it seems to be made up of two parts: **search** – meaning to look for something which is lost – and **re** – a Latin-derived prefix meaning, amongst other things, to do again. So, if you had never come across the composite word **research**, you might assume that it meant to repeatedly search for something lost.

The *Shorter Oxford Dictionary* tells us that it can be either a noun or a verb and gives, amongst a list of possible meanings, the following:

research
   (noun): the systematic study of materials and sources in order to establish facts and reach new conclusions.
   (verb): 1: to carry out systematic study of materials and sources in order to establish facts and reach new conclusions about something.
   2: to discover or verify information to be presented (in a book, programme, lecture, etc.).

In its broadest sense, 'research' includes any gathering of data, information and facts for the advancement of knowledge. Reading a factual book of any sort is a kind of research. Surfing the internet or watching the news is also sometimes considered to be a type of research. A scientist, though, would not use the word in this way. Scientists restrict it to certain narrowly defined areas – which I will discuss below – and use 'review' for the broad learning process which is an important part of uncovering knowledge.

A strict definition of scientific research is 'to perform a methodical study in order to prove an hypothesis or answer a specific question'. The central goal of any experimental process is to find a definitive answer to a preset question.

Scientific research – which in its modern form is a process developed during the Manhattan Project of World War II – must be systematic, follow a series of regular steps and meet a rigid standard protocol. (The rules are broadly similar but may vary slightly between different fields of science.) It must be organized and planned. It has to include a literature review of past research and an evaluation of the exact question to be answered.

This scientific definition seems to fit the word 'search', particularly if we are considering a search for an answer to a pre-set question. So to return to my original question: Why research?

When we consider the component parts of this word "re-search" they imply that we are talking about a search that is being repeated, and yet the dictionary definition says that it means "to reach new conclusions". The word embodies a verbal paradox. Its entomology suggests it is a repetition of a previous investigation whilst its definition says that it involves the discovery of new knowledge. I will return to this matter later in the chapter. But if we are going to study the nature and processes of research, we need to share a common understanding of the term before we start. The way you understand the word may be different from my intention when I use it. If I use the word research to imply a reviewing or revisiting of existing knowledge whilst you think it can only used in the context of searching for new knowledge we can easily end up at cross-purposes. Fortunately there is a simple way to resolve this matter by investigating what you intuitively think about the meaning of the word.

I have an understanding of the term which I will disclose later, but you will have your own inherent perception that you have grown up with and which has been reinforced by your education and culture. It is by no means certain that our two views will coincide so before we begin to look at the methodology and practice of "research" I want to help you to investigate your own perceptions of the meaning of the word. In due course I will explain my view.

Before I offer you my answer I want to ask you a question.

Are mathematical theories invented or discovered?

The answer you give to this question says a lot about how you view the nature of Truth.

Decide on your answer before turning the page.

HOW DO YOU THINK?

SORTING THE SHEEP FROM THE GOATS

Those of you who answered that mathematical theorems are 'invented' have been conditioned by your education to believe that all things have purposes which can be deduced by observation. You have a natural inclination towards a view of research that begins with observations and only then seeks to explain the observations by attributing causes to their invented purposes. I will return to this point later.

But those of you who answered that mathematical theorems are 'discovered' have a different view. You are the transcendental mystics of the business world. For a theorem to be discovered it must already exist before you have even thought about it.

Platonism

This idea of a transcendental world of absolute forms was proposed by the Greek philosopher Plato (427–347 BCE). He was the son of wealthy and influential Athenian parents and began his philosophical career as a student of Socrates. After Socrates was executed Plato travelled to Egypt and Italy, studied with the successors of Pythagoras and spent several years advising the ruling family of Syracuse. Eventually, he returned to Athens and established his own school of philosophy. Plato tried to pass on his heritage of a Socratic style of thinking and to guide his students' progress through mathematical learning to the achievement of abstract philosophical Truth.

Socrates had taught Plato that the most important varieties of human knowledge are really cases of recollection. Consider, for example, our knowledge of equality. We have no difficulty in deciding whether or not two people are perfectly equal in height. In fact, they are never exactly the same height, since we recognize that it would always be possible to discover some difference – however minute – with a more careful, precise measurement. By this standard, all the examples we perceive in ordinary life only approach, but never fully attain, perfect equality. But notice that, since we realize the Truth of this important qualification from our experience, we must somehow know for sure what true equality is, even though we have never seen it. Plato developed these ideas throughout his life (*Phaedo* 75b).

And he believed that the same point could be made with regard to other abstract concepts. Even though we perceive only their imperfect instances, we nonetheless have genuine knowledge of Truth, goodness and beauty, as well as of equality. Things of this sort are the Platonic Forms: abstract entities that exist independently of the sensible world. Ordinary objects are imperfect and changeable, but they faintly copy the perfect and immutable Forms. Thus, all the information we acquire about sensible objects (like knowing what proportion of the population prefers butter to margarine on its sandwiches) is temporary, insignificant and unreliable, while genuine knowledge of the Forms themselves (like knowing that $1 + 1 = 2$) is perfectly certain for ever.

Plato claimed that, since we have knowledge of these supra-sensible realities (knowledge that we cannot possibly have obtained through any bodily experience), it follows that this knowledge must be a form of recollection, and that our souls must have been acquainted with the Forms before birth. He believed the world was essentially intelligible, and so it must be the intellect and not the senses that had the ultimate 'vision' of this true being.

This vision of Platonic perfection drives all scientists and is at the heart of all systems of scientific research which have been developed in the twentieth century. This is the Research system we are going to study.

As Roger Penrose, a committed Scientific Platonist, says:

> The Platonic viewpoint is an immensely valuable one. It tells us to be careful to distinguish the precise mathematical entities from the approximations that we see around us in the world of physical things. Moreover, it provides us with the blueprint according to which modern science has proceeded. Scientists will put forward models of the world – or, rather, of certain aspects of the world – and these models may be tested against previous observation and against the results of carefully designed experiment. The models are deemed to be appropriate if they survive rigorous examination and if, in addition, they are internally consistent structures. The important point about these models is that they are basically purely abstract mathematical models. The very

question of the internal consistency of a scientific model, in particular, is one that requires that the model be precisely specified. The required precision demands that the model be a mathematical one, for otherwise one cannot be sure that these questions have well-defined answers.

If the model itself is to be assigned any kind of 'existence', then this existence is located within the Platonic world of mathematical forms. Of course, one might take a contrary viewpoint: namely that the model is itself to have existence only within our various minds, rather than to take Plato's world to be in any sense absolute and 'real'. Yet, there is something important to be gained in regarding mathematical structures as having a reality of their own. For our individual minds are notoriously imprecise, unreliable and inconsistent in their judgments. The precision, reliability, and consistency that are required by our scientific theories demand something beyond any one of our individual (untrustworthy) minds. In mathematics, we find a far greater robustness than can be located in any particular mind. Does this not point to something outside ourselves, with a reality that lies beyond what each individual can achieve?

(Penrose 2004)

The Platonist philosophy, which underlies the scientific method of answering questions about reality, gives rise to the term 're-search'. As a scientist, Penrose, when he conducts Re-Search, is repeating a search, one which any individual can repeat independently, to discover a Truth about the mathematical nature of reality.

This form of research was formalized during World War II, when scientists working for the Allies – in particular Leo Szilard and Albert Einstein in the US (DeGroot 2004) and Neils Bohr in the UK – realized that there was a distinct possibility that a weapon of immense destructive power already existed within the realms of Platonic Truth. The implication of this thought was that the weapon was sitting there waiting for the first bold searcher to discover it and apply it to winning the war. That searcher could be on either side. Basic work on nuclear instability had been carried out by Heisenberg but was ignored by Hitler. In the UK work on material preparation for a ballistic-impact uranium bomb was already well under way at the Nobel explosive works in Porth Madog, North Wales, under the secret patronage of the MAUD committee (Zimmerman 1996). This fearsome weapon was sitting, unprotected, in the realm of the Platonic Forms waiting to be discovered. Szilard and Einstein wrote to President Roosevelt urging him to devote all the US's scientific talent to the search, suggesting that the consequences of Hitler getting there first would be catastrophic (DeGroot 2004).

Roosevelt took heed of their warning and set up the Manhattan Project. It brought together the organizational and logistic skills of Gen. Leslie Groves and the inspired scientific leadership of Dr J. Robert Oppenheimer in the remote desert site of Los Alamos. The result was two types of atom bomb, one based on uranium (Little Boy) and one based on plutonium (Fat Boy). Both designs worked, and both were deployed over Japanese cities. A major spin-off of this massive wartime effort, for our purposes, was a new method for conducting research (Hughes 2002).

It is that method of research, which underlies most of the standard textbooks on Research Methods. The Platonists among you will be completely comfortable with this approach.

But what of those who answered that mathematical theorems are 'invented'? They are following a different philosophy.

Aristotelianism

Those who think mathematical theorems are invented are subscribing to a view of reality which believes that everything can be understood by observing reality and then thinking about the purposes of the objects they have seen.

This view was first put forward by another Greek philosopher, Aristotle (384–322 BCE). He was born at Stagira in northern Greece and is the most notable product of the educational programme devised by Plato; he spent twenty years studying at Plato's Academy. When Plato died, Aristotle returned to his native Macedonia, where he is supposed to have participated in the education of King Philip of Macedon's son, Alexander (the Great). He returned to Athens with Alexander's approval in 335 and established his own school at the Lyceum, spending most of the rest of his life engaged there in research, teaching and writing. His students acquired the name 'Peripatetics' from the master's habit of strolling about as he taught. The aim of Aristotle's logical treatises (known collectively as the *Organon*) was to develop a universal method of reasoning by means of which it would be possible to learn everything there is to know about reality.

Aristotle said that everything has four purposes, or causes, associated with it. These purposes can be deduced from observing the objects and thinking about why they were invented.

Here they are:

1. **The Material cause:** 'that from which a thing comes to be made: e.g. bronze would be a cause of a statue'. This Material cause explains the physical composition.

   An object comes into existence due to its parts, constituents, substratum or materials. Aristotle gives as an example the production of an artefact like a bronze statue; the bronze is considered the Material cause. In this example, the bronze has to undergo a change before it results in a statue. It must be melted and poured into a wax cast to acquire the desired shape: that of a statue.

2. **The Formal cause:** 'the form, or pattern . . . the form is an account of the essence . . . and the parts of the account'. This is the design or shape of the object.

   The Formal cause pertains to the essence or 'pattern' of something. It simply points out to us what a thing is, so that any thing may be identified by the 'definition, form, pattern, essence, whole, synthesis or archetype'. For instance, the Formal cause of a statue of a person is what it has to be in order to be so called: it must have a head, be a certain length and portray a recognizable person. This shape is part of the explanation of the production of the statue and was invented by the sculptor.

3. **The Efficient cause:** 'the source of the primary principle of change or stability': e.g. the sculptor who conceives the shape of the statue. 'The producer is a cause of the product, and the initiator of the change is a cause of what is changed.'

   The Efficient cause, according to Aristotle, explains a thing in terms of its starting point of change or stability. Aristotle pointed out that Efficient cause is 'the primary source of change'. The Efficient cause implies all agents of change, whether non-living or living. The Efficient cause of the statue was the sculptor – the person who made the change in the bronze, turning it into a statue. But an in-depth review of the production of a statue points to a deeper Efficient cause or principle that produces it. Aristotle believes it is not just the artist but the art of bronze-casting statues which brings it about. Aristotle believes an artisan merely manifests knowledge in the production of the statue. It is this knowledge of statue production, not the artisan who has mastered it, that is the fullest depiction of the Efficient cause.

4. **The Final cause:** 'something's end (*telos*) – i.e. what it is for – is its cause, as good health is caused by walking'.

   The Final cause explains something in terms of its purpose, why it is made. According to Aristotle, the Final cause is that for the sake of which a thing exists or is done, its purpose and instrumental actions and activities – the end which something must serve. For example, the Final cause of a statue could be to portray a goddess or to act as a decoration, or both. Each step of the artistic sculpting process leads to that final cause for the sake of which everything has been done.

The 'four causes' provide answers to four questions you might ask about anything. For example, about a part-time MBA student:

Q. What is it made from?
A. Flesh, blood and bone (Material cause).
Q. What is its form or essence?
A. A two-legged, two-armed, one-headed creature capable of reasoned thought (Formal cause).
Q. What produced it?
A. Its father and mother acting on the impulses of biology (Efficient cause).
Q. For what purpose?
A. To live a fulfilling and happy life in accordance with its reasoned impulses (Final cause).

Platonists will find statistics, hypothesis-testing and business modelling a comfortable approach to business research, whilst Aristotelians will tend to prefer market research and case studies.

Any type of 'real' research – whether scientific, economic, historical or business – requires some kind of interpretation and an opinion from the researcher. This opinion is the underlying principle that is set by the question you ask. That question establishes the nature and type of experiment. Your philosophical inclination will greatly affect the sort of questions you pose and the way you try to answer them. Trying to fight your natural inclination seldom leads to good research, persuasive arguments or successful dissertations.

WORKING TO YOUR STRENGTHS

But let us not forget that the purpose of this little book it to help you learn how to carry out research and write up a business management project.

Researching and writing a dissertation involves a number of steps, and the sequence of steps will be different for Platonists and Aristotelians.

Platonist Sequence	**Aristotelian Sequence**
1. Identify an interesting business or management problem.	1. Identify an interesting business or management problem.
2. Pose a realistic question about the problem.	2. Pose a realistic question about the problem.
3. Review the literature about the problem and see if anybody has already discovered a solution to the problem which can be applied.	3. Observe the features and players involved in the problem and write down what you see happening. This stage may also involve collecting facts and figures about the problem.
4. Decide what new information you need to collect and how you will obtain it.	4. Try to identify and justify motives and causes for the actions you have observed and recorded.

5. Set up a model or hypothesis which can be tested to prove or disprove your findings.

5. Review the literature to see if others have noted similar motives and causes in similar circumstances.

6. Collect your data.

6. Answer the question based on your own experience compared to the literature.

7. Test the model against the new data and answer the question.

7. Write up the results. (This step breaks down into another sequence, which I will discuss later in the book.)

8. Write up the results. (This step breaks down into another sequence, which I will discuss later in the book.)

You will notice that the first two steps are identical, no matter what your philosophy, and the final writing process will also be the same for all. What differs between the two approaches is the order of doing things and the tools you might choose to use.

The key to successful dissertation-writing lies in picking a problem that interests and motivates you, and then asking a good, insightful question about it. The task of writing then becomes simple. First state your question, justifying why it matters; then answer it in a complete, persuasive and logical manner.

To help you think about the nature of business problems, my Platonist definition is 'an objective to be met and a choice of means of reaching that objective'.

Without both an objective and a choice of means there is no problem, because there is no way of changing the outcome. Management is the art of the possible, not a search for some general Truth about life. Without a business objective and a choice of actions there is nothing you can do to change things; hence there is no problem to study, and nothing sensible to write up for your dissertation. Choose your problem by applying careful thought – it is the most important step in dissertation-writing.

To understand your objective it is important to state your problem in clear, unambiguous terms. If your problem is choosing what shoes to wear, then you must decide what objective you are seeking to meet. Is it:

- to keep your feet dry?
- to impress a potential employer at an interview?
- to protect your feet from rough ground or dropped tools?
- to aid your running prowess?

Having clarified your objective, the next step is to list all the possible choices. What shoes do you have in your wardrobe? (If you only have one pair of shoes you don't have a problem.) Once you have listed all the alternatives, the solution of the problem consists in evaluating the alternatives in order to choose the one that best satisfies your objective.

This is an easy sequence to see but can involve quite a lot of detailed work to carry it out. The list of alternatives may be long, the choice may not be clear-cut, but the need for information and a systematic approach to the task is always going to be important. Over the next few chapters we will look at methods and techniques of deriving and using information.

The difficult part of dissertation production is deciding what question(s) you need to ask in order to bring out the key features of your selected problem. I suggest you begin your private study with a study of business questions.

FORMING A STUDY GROUP AND KEEPING A LEARNING LOG

To gain the maximum benefit from this book, I suggest you form a study group with a few other students (no more than five others, if available, although just a single fellow traveller can be a great aid to discussion). After each chapter I will suggest discussion topics for your study group. You should keep notes on these discussions, along with your own thoughts about the topics I have raised in each chapter.

The written assignment, set out below, should be incorporated into your Learning Log. This is a journal that you keep to record your thoughts and acquisition of facts as they occur. When you come upon a useful insight, make a note of it. When you struggle to understand, make a note of what puzzles you and then bring it as a question to your tutor. Each time you work on the topic, make sure you write down your impressions, confusion, discoveries and facts while they are fresh in your mind. The resulting set of notes will help you reflect on the learning process and help you understand how you learn.

At Bradford we allow our students to take their Learning Logs into the exam, where it often proves to be a most helpful summary of what a student needs to know.

GROUP DISCUSSION TOPIC FOR CHAPTER 1

What is the purpose of a business dissertation from the point of view of:

1. The Student?
2. The business the Student wants to work in?
3. The university to which the dissertation will be submitted?

WRITTEN EXERCISE

(To be conducted individually and brought to the study group for discussion)

Set aside four hours of continuous uninterrupted free time. Then sit down and write about the following topics, taking at least 500 words in total.

1. Identify and describe a business problem which interests you.
2. Explain why the problem matters to you and your business.
3. Pose an insightful question about the problem – one that you feel you will be able to answer within the word limits set for your dissertation.
4. Outline what you will need to do to answer your question.

Chapter

2

WHERE DO YOU START?

STAKEHOLDERS, PROBLEMS AND CHOICES

W HEN FACED WITH THE ISSUE of deciding on a topic for a dissertation most students struggle. A popular response is to procrastinate and, when pressed, retreat into formulaic and meaningless waffle. Yet selecting a dissertation topic is one of the most potentially empowering steps towards mastering business skills that a manager can take. When you choose the direction research for your dissertation will take, you are either embarking on a self-development process that will transform your managerial life, or you are taking on a chore which could make you despair of ever finishing.

A common feature of successful dissertations is a careful choice of problem to research. But this choice is not straightforward, for several reasons:

- There are a number of stakeholders to consider.
- The range of possible problems seems infinite.
- You have to produce a large number of sensible, well-reasoned words against a deadline.

In this chapter I intend to look at each of these issues in turn.

Let's begin with the main stakeholders. Supporting the bottom of this triad of self-interest is the **Student**: the one who has to pose the questions, understand the problem, collect the facts and arrive at sensible conclusions. Here are some possible motivations for students.

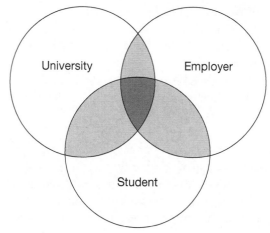

Figure 2.1
The Main Stakeholders in a Successful Dissertation

- to obtain a degree;
- to gain a passport that can open doors to new areas of employment or promotion;
- to increase earnings;
- to get the best possible mark for the least possible work;
- to demonstrate knowledge and understanding, and so become respected;
- to learn about the chosen business problem;
- to learn to successfully adapt to new circumstances;
- to learn about themselves.

The **University's** motives will be different. Possibilities include:

- to be able to award an appropriate degree to a successful candidate;
- to ensure that students develop and demonstrate useful business skills;
- to maintain academic standards and pass on accumulated know-ledge to the next generation of managers;
- to help students learn how to learn, so that they can successfully adapt to new circumstances;
- to help students gain a passport that opens doors to new areas of employment or promotion, so that they become respected Alumni

of the University and become part of the University's business network;

- to network with local employers and enlist their goodwill in providing future students;
- to maintain the good name and reputation of the University, so as to achieve good rankings and future students (thus ensuring future revenue streams).

Some students are self-funded or family-funded (in which case the role of the employer may be filled by the bank manager who lends the money, the wife who agrees to the use of savings, the Bank of Mum and Dad who sponsor the adventure, or the conscience of the individual who dips into his/her own pocket). But many are sponsored to undertake their degree by their current employer. It is the motives of such an **Employer,** or altruistic sponsor, I will consider next. These may include:

- to create staff with appropriate postgraduate degrees;
- to improve their staff's management skills;
- to use the incentive of sponsorship to retain staff who might otherwise move on – which can work in two ways:
  - through golden handcuffs (you agree to stay with the employer for a fixed number of years after graduating);
  - through increasing job satisfaction and providing skilled candidates for internal promotion;
- to create a pool of staff who know how to learn, and can adapt to new circumstances rapidly and effectively;
- to obtain cheap, yet knowledgeable, management consultancy by means of supervised and guided research conducted by an individual with an in-depth knowledge of their firm;
- to increase the long-term profitability of the company by ensuring it is well managed;
- to tap into academic sources of information which would be extremely expensive to procure commercially;
- to improve the knowledge base of the firm.

Figure 2.1 shows that all these motives split into areas of possible agreement and possible conflict. The strategic choice of problem and the tactical decisions about specific research questions can circumvent zones of conflict or pitch the student into them; this should be borne in mind when considering suitable problems. Conflict is possible in the white areas of the diagram, where one stakeholder's motives are not shared by any of the others, and also in the grey areas, where the interests of two stakeholders coincide but are not shared by the third. For instance:

- The University may be keen to network with a local Employer, and so be inclined to offer 'cheap, yet knowledgeable, management consultancy, by means of supervised and guided research conducted by an individual with an in-depth knowledge of their firm'. But the Student may not be interested in the problem that engages the Employer and the University.

Or

- The University may encourage a Student who would like to research a particular problem of business theory that is currently fashionable in academic journals but has no practical interest for the Employer.

Or

- The Employer and the Student, for sound commercial reasons, may want to research a problem the University regards as academically trivial and of insufficient intellectual content to be worthy of a degree dissertation.

There is little potential conflict in the black areas, where all three stakeholders agree that it is desirable:

- To obtain a degree.
- To improve the student's skill level.
- To make the student a more attractive candidate for promotion (though the Employer will naturally consider internal promotion more desirable than external advancement).

From this brief overview it should be clear that choice of business problem is a key strategic decision. Some 2,500 years ago the great Chinese general Sun Tzu pointed out:

> Great Warriors first make themselves invincible. Then they await the enemy's moment of vulnerability. Not to be conquered depends on oneself, to conquer depends on the actions of the enemy; thus a skilled warrior can always remain unvanquished. But the enemy may not be vulnerable, therefore one who cannot conquer defends, but one who can conquer attacks.
>
> > (*The Art of War*, annotated by the warlord Cao Cao, cited in Krause 1996)

Choose your problem with a view to making sure you gain the maximum benefit from it, whilst not leaving yourself open to criticism by either your employer or your supervisor – or, even worse, creating a real possibility of failing. However, you must understand the nature of business problems, before you can exercise good judgment in your choices.

A SIMPLE TAXONOMY OF BUSINESS PROBLEMS

Business problems break down in four major groupings:

- problems of observation;
- problems of prediction;
- problems of planning;
- problems of business theory.

The first three are Aristotelian in nature, the fourth Platonic.

Before breaking down these major phyla into distinct classes of problems, it will be useful to look more closely at the Aristotelian and Platonic methods of research. These will affect your approach to answering the questions you are able to pose about different types of problem.

A basic requirement for all research, Platonic or Aristotelian, is to demonstrate the testability of the findings. To establish a Platonic

Truth we have to be able to determine whether our hypotheses are definitely wrong or possibly correct (I suggest you leave statements of certainty to preachers and politicians). I will return to Platonic Research methods later in this chapter.

AN ARISTOTELIAN APPROACH

The richness of business observation may push you to use different methods of testing, but testability has to remain a basic requirement of any acceptable research methodology. We may choose to work with rich and diverse data concerning the consequences of past business events, but rarely are we able to infer from these observations Platonic laws of general business behaviour. We search for repeated patterns, hoping to find evidence so abundant and so diverse that no other co-ordinating interpretation could possibly be accepted, even though any single item might not be enough to provide conclusive proof.

The great nineteenth-century philosopher of science William Whewell devised the word **consilience**, meaning 'jumping together', to designate the confidence gained when many independent sources 'conspire' to indicate a particular historical pattern. He called the strategy of co-ordinating disparate results from multifarious sources 'consilience of induction' (Wilson 1998).

Charles Darwin is one of the greatest of all Aristotelian scientists. He developed convincing evidence for evolution as the co-ordinating principle of life's history, but he also chose as a central theme for his writings the development of a rigorous Aristotelian methodology to utilize observation in research (Gould 1986). Darwin explored a variety of modes of narrative historical explanation, each appropriate for differing densities of preserved information (Gould 1986: 60–64), but his central argument rested on the concept of consilience. He maintained that we know evolution must underlie the order of life because no other explanation can co-ordinate the disparate data of embryology, biogeography, the fossil record, vestigial organs, taxonomic relationships, and so on. Darwin explicitly rejected the notion that a cause must be seen directly in order to qualify as a scientific explanation. Instead he wrote about the proper testing of natural selection, invoking the idea of consilience to create an observation-based explanation (Darwin 1998).

But Aristotelian researchers must go beyond the simple demonstration that their explanations can be tested by equally rigorous procedures different from the stereotype of the Platonic method. They must also convince their **employer** and the **university** that explanations of this observational type are both interesting, informative and academically valid.

Aristotelian explanations take the form of a narrative: P, the phenomenon to be explained, arose because Z came before, preceded by W, X and Y. If any of these earlier stages had not occurred, or had happened differently, then P would not exist (or would be present in a substantially altered form, Q, requiring a different explanation or sequence of causes). Thus, P makes sense and can be explained rigorously as the outcome of W through Y. But no law of nature caused P; any variant Q arising from an altered set of antecedents could have been equally explicable, though massively different in form and effect.

This is not to say that business research is the study of randomness. We can show by the use of a detailed case study that P had to arise, as a consequence of W through Z. But the actual outcome was a result of contingency.[1] An historical observational explanation does not rest on direct deductions from laws of nature, but on an unpredictable sequence of preceding states, where any major change in the sequence alters the final result. This final result is therefore contingent upon everything that came before. If you could rerun the sequence of events, then you would be likely to get a different result. There is no Platonic Truth underlying this one-off outcome, and it is unlikely that it will be possible to demonstrate repeatability of outcome for a given set of inputs.

For the Platonist, schooled in the archetype of the scientific method, such Aristotelian contingent explanations seem less interesting or less scientific, even when their appropriateness and essential correctness have to be admitted. Suppose we have collected a set of historical explanations about the outcome of a business problem, as well documented as anything in Platonic science. These results did not arise as deducible consequences from any Platonic law of nature; they were not even predictable from any general or abstract property of the larger

---

1   A contingent proposition is not necessarily either true or false. It is contingent because it contains logical links between facts, which show it to be true in any particular case.

business system (such as superiority in market share or attractiveness of product offering). But I would argue that these Aristotelian assessments of problems can be as interesting and important as a conventional scientific conclusion. The documentation of evidence, and the probability of discovering Truth by disproof of alternatives, may be every bit as conclusive as any Platonic explanation. And if the current taxonomic order and relative diversity of business life are simply a consequence of random historical events, rather than a potential deduction from general evolutionary business pressures, then contingency might be a basic pattern of nature, and an understanding of its processes a desirable managerial skill.

Finally, case studies can be endlessly fascinating in themselves, in many ways more intriguing to the human psyche than the inexorable consequences of nature's laws. We are especially moved by events that did not have to be, but that occurred for identifiable reasons subject to incessant mulling and stewing. (Note the endless speculation about how the recent banking crisis might have been avoided.) By contrast, both the extreme views of Platonism – the inevitable (Newtonian) and the truly random (Quantum) – make less impact on our emotions because they cannot be controlled by history's agents and objects. Such problems cannot be managed and therefore have to be endured. But, with contingency, we are drawn in; we become involved; we share the pain of triumph or tragedy. When we realize that the actual outcome did not have to be, that any alteration in any step along the way would have unleashed a whole different outcome, we grasp the causal power of individual events and the value of managerial intervention. We can argue, lament or exult over each detail, because each holds the possibility of transformation. Contingency is an affirmation of control by the minutiae of immediate events over the grand pattern of destiny – the kingdom lost for want of a horseshoe nail. It gives us the hope that, if we can manage to sustain the supply of horseshoe nails, then we can win the war.

A PLATONIST APPROACH

Modern science follows a systematic procedure for developing its ideas, based on a concept of the Platonic Truth of mathematical models. These ideas first appeared in the seventeenth century in Restoration England, and they underpinned the long-term success of the newly formed Royal Society.

There are three important steps in this process: observation, prediction and control.

First you observe the phenomenon you are trying to explain, name its parts, describe its functions and make sure that you can record exactly what happens. Sometimes this step will involve developing new measuring instruments, such as telescopes to view the stars, microscopes to observe the detail of cells, or questionnaires to collect information. Sometimes it might involve making a more accurate clock to count fractions of a second, or a more accurate calendar to time the years and the seasons. Often it will involve carrying out experiments to see what will happen – like pumping away the air from around a man's arm to see if it swells up, or stuffing snow into a dead chicken to see if it rots more slowly: experiments carried out in the seventeenth century by Robert Hooke and Francis Bacon respectively (Lomas 2009). It might involve collecting and classifying plants into different types, which can then be named, or seeing if trees grow faster when their roots are sprinkled with saltpetre. The founders of the Royal Society did all these things, and more, at a time when most 'scholars' never bothered to observe anything, and they began the movement towards modern formalized research.

Descartes, the philosopher who was a contemporary of many of these founders, based his system of mechanics on two principles which he held to be Platonic Truths: the identification of space with matter and a view of motion which only allowed for moving bodies to move from contact with one body in order to make contact with another. His view of space has survived with his system of Cartesian co-ordinates which is a method where any point in space can be described by counting along two (or three) axes at right angles to each other (perhaps the best-known example is the way is describing the position of a piece on a chessboard by counting the rows and columns). But his ideas on motion have not survived as Platonic Truths. He said that a body only moved in order to make contact with another body, so the opposite of motion is rest, and all motions result in impacts between bodies. (Try telling that to the snooker-player whose attempt to pot the final black turned into a non-contacting foul stroke!) But

Descartes never let observation get in the way of a good theory, even when the theory was wrong.

As the new observational attitude to science spread throughout the academic community, promoted by the Royal Society, scientists took advantage of their new-found freedom to look at things which religion had previously held sacred. For example, Thomas Willis explored the anatomy of the brains of his patients who died, and founded the modern science of neurology.

The fundamental change in attitude towards using observation to test Platonic Truths, which the Royal Society brought about, can be seen in 1668, when John Wallis, Christopher Wren and Christiaan Huygens were asked by the Royal Society to devise a mathematical method for working out the motion of projectiles. Wallis, perhaps the most celebrated of all theoretical thinkers of the time, and the father of modern algebra, wrote when accepting the commission, 'Experiment will be the best judge of our deliberations.' This was put into practice when King Charles asked them to investigate why, when a frog was put into a brimming glass of water the glass did not overflow. The premise was quickly and empirically disproved by putting a frog in a glass of water and noting that the glass *did* overflow! (Lomas 2009).

After observation, the next stage of the classical research process is prediction. Here it is necessary to build a theoretical (usually mathematical or statistical) model to explain the observations, and then to use it to predict the outcome of an as-yet-untried experiment. If the prediction is accurate, the model can be considered to be a reasonable representation, but if the model fails to predict the outcome, then it must be replaced or rebuilt until the outcome can be predicted. It is a harsh reality of this research method that, no matter how many times a model has worked in the past, if it fails once, it is wrong and should be discarded or changed. I must add here that this is a counsel of perfection and does not always happen; researchers, being only human, hate discarding old, comfortable and familiar theories.

The first modern researchers of the Royal Society put forward predictions and tested them against reality. They built diving bells, twin-hulled ships, wind-driven carriages, spring-driven clocks and new sorts of pistols to test the predictions of their new theories. Perhaps the most famous example of the application of this principle of observation followed by prediction is the story of Halley's Comet.

Before the founding of the Royal Society, comets were not understood. By fostering the development of accurate telescopes, precise clocks and systematic recording of observations, the Fellows of the society built up a database of sightings of comets. From the detail of the directions of the sighting they created theories of how comets moved until, finally, Edmund Halley, using the observations of John Flamsteed, and the gravitational theories of Isaac Newton, predicted the regular return of the comet which bears his name.

The final objective of this type of research is control. The accepted view is that, once you can describe a process and can predict its outcomes, you can then hope to intervene and adjust the outcomes to be as you want them. This is the step of control. Modern science has given us such a high degree of mastery over our world that we have almost forgotten what the pre-scientific world was like. When Robert Hooke first started to draw the minute creatures he saw through his microscope he was astonished at what he saw. He amused his noble sponsors by supplying them with drawings of the tiny creatures he observed through his eyepiece, and so helped keep the funds flowing. However, while making these amusing drawings, he was looking closely at plants and at human skin and saw tiny subdivisions in the basic structure. He described these as looking like small cells of monks, grouping together to form a cloister (hence the name 'cell' for a basic unit of biological life) – the first step on the road towards the cloning of living beings had been taken. Hence the study of biological cells stretches directly back to Hooke in the seventeenth century and his first microscopic studies of tissue. His observation of the basic biological unit still echoes through the literature of science, surviving in his metaphor for the spaces he saw in living tissue as 'cells' (meaning small empty rooms). Hooke went on to produce a series of detailed micrographic drawings of small creatures and published them in a book entitled *Micrographia*, which contains some of the most beautiful drawings of insects and the minute structure of feathers and fish scales ever seen (Hooke 2007). Later scientists predicted how these cells could be manipulated, and, eventually, Wilmut and Campbell achieved control of the technology of 'cells' and created Dolly, the first cloned sheep (Wilmut *et al.* 2000).

Now let us consider the types of problems normally encountered in business.

PROBLEMS OF OBSERVATION

This is a group of problems which occur when little is known about an area of business and the issue is how to find out what is happening. Typical examples of this type of problems can be broken down into the following classes (you may care to add to the list):

- How to determine how a market works.
- How to understand how a complex organization is actually functioning.
- How to discover the extent of competition in a market.
- How to discover the size of a potential market.
- Studies of consumer behaviour.

PROBLEMS OF PREDICTION

The problems in this group are all concerned with the best ways to foresee the future prospects of a business (again, you may like to add to this list):

- Will a new product succeed?
- Can a successful new business be set up?
- Is it worth an existing firm entering a different market?
- What will happen if I start a new career?
- Will changes in public opinion affect the way a firm can do business?
- Will changes in the law or the regulatory environment affect the way a firm has to do business?
- Can a firm improve its performance in a particular area by changing its way of working? (This might be in any business area, such as finance, human relations, organizational structure, innovation, marketing, operations, forecasting or market intelligence.)

PROBLEMS OF PLANNING

These are concerned with looking at ways to bring about changes in a business (once more, you might like to add to the list):

- How should a new way of working be introduced into a business or into any part of it?
- How can a firm adjust to changes in its market?
- How can a firm adjust to meet new regulations?
- How can a firm adopt new technology?
- How can a firm adapt to changes in public attitudes?

PROBLEMS OF BUSINESS THEORY

This group is concerned with testing business theories against the reality of business life.

- Is a particular piece of business or economic theory confirmed by reality?
- Can a piece of business theory be used by a firm?
- How can a new business theory be developed and tested?

Each of these types of problem poses different issues when you try to research it. The nature of the research issues will also depend on the exact form of the question the researcher chooses to ask about the problem. The first step is to produce a list of possible questions about your chosen problem so that you can make a reasoned choice among the alternatives.

GROUP DISCUSSION TOPIC FOR CHAPTER 2

Take your written assessment of problems, questions and plans for answering them and discuss with your study group. Use the following questions to spark off your discussion.

- Is your problem clear, well-defined and important? Could the statement be improved?
- Is the question you are planning to ask practical within the limits of time and word count. Could it be improved?
- Is your plan for trying to answer the question well thought out, and does it lead you to a plan of action with well-defined milestones?

Take notes on the discussion to add to your Learning Log.

3

HAS SOMEBODY ANSWERED MY QUESTION BEFORE?

TAPPING THE CORNUCOPIA OF INFORMATION AND POSSIBILITIES

O NCE YOU KNOW THE NATURE of your problem, and have made a list of possible questions, then the next step is to find out if somebody has already invented, or discovered, an answer to your question or a similar question.

This involves looking at the literature to see what is already written about the topic. This prior knowledge is stored in a different taxonomical form from the way we have grouped our problems. Topic knowledge is stored by academic business discipline. Here are the main disciplines of business in alphabetical order.

- Accounting
- Business Finance
- Contracts
- Economics
- Industrial Management
- Information Systems
- Information Technology
- Law
- Marketing
- Organization & Management
- Purchasing
- Quantitative Methods

Each discipline can be subdivided into their main subject areas, thus:

Accounting

- Cost Accounting Standards
- Cost Accounting Technique
- Management Accounting Technique

Business Finance

- Business Communications
- Business and Personnel Management
- Business Statistics
- Cost Analysis
- Financial Cost Management
- Financial Planning and Analysis
- Inventory Management
- Resource Planning
- Risk Analysis

Contracts

- Acquisition Contracting
- Acquisition Management
- Business Communications in Contracting Writing
- Business Contract Law
- Contract Administration
- Contract Law
- Contract Management
- Contract Pricing and Negotiation
- Contracting Management
- Cost & Price Analysis
- Government Contracting
- Government Contract Law
- Procurement Standards
- Procurement and Contracting
- Procurement Management

Economics

- Cost Analysis
- Cost and Price Analysis
- Economic Analysis
- Economic Principles and Decision Making
- Economics and Financial Management
- Economics Theory

Industrial Management

- Automated Systems in Logistics Management
- Civil Engineering Management
- Engineering and Analysis
- Environmental Management
- Logistics Management
- Logistics and Material Management
- Manufacturing Management
- Material Acquisition Process & Support Systems
- Property Disposal Management
- Supply Management
- Systems Engineering Technology
- Systems Management
- Warehousing Operations

Information Systems

- Business Intelligence Systems
- Decision Support Systems
- Expert Systems
- Information Systems Development
- Information Systems Management
- Information Systems Security
- Information Systems Strategy
- Management Information Systems
- Office Automation Systems
- Transaction Processing Systems

Information Technology

- Communications
- Interface Design
- Network Design
- Network Strategy
- Platform and Server Strategy
- Web Design

Law

- Commercial or Business Contracts
- Contract Law
- Ethics

Marketing

- Advertising
- Distribution and Logistics
- Market Forecasting
- Market Research
- Product Development and Innovation
- Promotion
- Selling

Organization & Management

- Business Administration
- Business Management
- Business Strategy
- General Management
- Human Resource Development
- Leadership and Group Decision Process
- Management & Leadership
- Management Science
- Managerial Analysis
- Manpower Management
- Material Management

- Organizational Behaviour
- Personnel Administration
- Personnel Management
- Principles of Management
- Quality and Reliability
- Research & Development Management
- Strategic Management
- Systems Development

Purchasing

- Basic Purchasing Technique
- Procurement Strategy
- Procurement Management
- Supply Chain Management

Quantitative Methods

- Business Statistics
- Decision Risk Analysis
- Operations Research
- Probability Statistics
- Qualitative Analysis
- Quantitative Analysis
- Statistical Theory

This is a wide range of disciplines encompassing an even wider range of topics. Your problem is where to start your search for useful pre-existing knowledge of your chosen problem.

You will have noticed that, although the taxonomy of academic knowledge is organized differently to the outline taxonomy of problems, there is a lot of overlap. This means that to begin your research you will need to know two things. The first is which academic disciplines address the essence of your problem; this will enable you to see if there is any pre-existing theory you can apply. The second is the actual question you want to address; this will help you find any pertinent data.

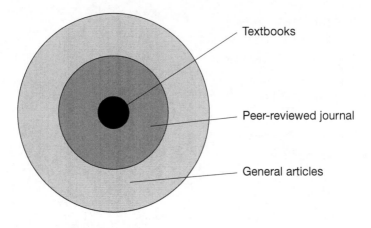

Figure 3.1
The Fuzzy Structure of Academic Literature

UNTANGLING THE FUZZY BALL OF KNOWLEDGE

In general a subject will have a central core of well-accepted data, which will be in the form of textbooks – around this will be a fringe of peer-reviewed research journals, which in turn are surrounded by a wider mantle of general articles and studies, often written by practitioners (see Figure 3.1). As you move away from the core the material tends to become more speculative, more nebulous – but also more up-to-date.

A good place to start is with the most recent textbooks on the subject. These can be found by searching your university library catalogue.

Say, for example, your problem is 'How to discover the size of a potential market'. The main tool you will need to use will be Market Research. A good place to start will be the section in the library which houses textbooks on your chosen topic.

If you enter the key words 'Market Research' into the Library catalogue for Bradford University Library, this will return a list of 713 titles for current textbooks on Market Research. Obviously this is far too many to read for inspiration, so they need to be sorted. There appear to be two practical choices.

BY RELEVANCE

When I checked, the top book by this criterion at Bradford was:

Market Research in Practice: A guide to the basics / Paul Hague, Nick Hague and Carol-Ann Morgan

Clicking on the entry gives more detail about the contents:

Contents Introduction – Market research design – Desk research – Focus groups – Depth interviewing – Observation – Sampling and statistics – Questionnaire design – Face-to-face interviewing – Telephone interviewing – Self-completion questionnaires – E-surveys – Data analysis – Reporting.

The system also lets you know where to find it (Management Library – Main - E 658.83 HAG), that it can be borrowed for up to four weeks, and whether it is currently available.

BY DATE OF PUBLICATION

If you re-sort the library search list by date you will get the most recent publications on the library shelf that include the search keywords in their abstract.

When I did this for 'Market Research' I got:

'The reconfiguration of the state in an era of neoliberal globalism: State violence and indigenous responses in the Costa Chica-Montaña of Guerrero, Mexico'.

This was a thesis by L.P. Parra-Rosales which had just been accepted into the Library. While you may occasionally be lucky and get the most recently added textbook on your subject, this is a more likely outcome with most university library systems.

A better way to find the most recent title in your subject area on the library shelf is first to search by relevance and then narrow it down, using year of publication, until you find a textbook on your chosen subject.

When I did this I found the most recent textbook on Market Research was:

The Practice of Market and Social Research: An introduction / Yvonne McGivern

which was published in 2006. The additional detail about it was:

Marketing research. Marketing research – Methodology. Social sciences – Research.
Social sciences – Research – Methodology.

Its location was given as

Management Library – Main – E 658.83 MAC

and it could be borrowed for one week.

But now we know that the textbooks on Market Research are to be found at shelf location E 658.83, and at this point I would recommend going along to the shelf and looking through the books available to see which are most helpful in getting you started.

USING AMAZON

A practical suggestion for finding the most recent textbook is to search for your topic of interest (e.g. Market Research) on Amazon and then sort the list by date of publication. It will be bound to give you many 'not yet published' books, but if you skim down you can find the most recent in print. When I did this I found

Marketing Research: An applied orientation (paperback) by Naresh K. Malhotra

published by Pearson Education in its sixth edition on 1 October 2009.

USING THE BRITISH LIBRARY CATALOGUE

The website for the British Library is

http://www.bl.uk/

and its integrated catalogue search facility is at

http://catalogue.bl.uk/F/?func=file&file_name=login-bl-list

This can be helpful when searching for information on unusual and obscure problems about which there are no current textbooks.

Once you have looked at the textbook view of the academic discipline which relates to your problem you need to get more specific in your searching. At this point you need to move away from the solid centre of the diagram and the textbooks on the library shelf, and move towards the outer perimeter of peer-reviewed journals (see Figure 3.1 pg. 32). Now more general search tools must be brought to bear.

USING METALIB TO SEARCH FOR DATA ON SPECIFIC PROBLEMS

The Metalib search engine can be accessed through your university portal and gives access to a whole raft of data. (Your university library will provide you with a password and basic instructions on how to operate the search engine.)

Let us say that your particular sub-question (probably part of a bigger question about the strategy of petrol retailing or the logistical issues of haulage businesses) relates to the impact of fuel prices on the retail petrol market. For example: 'What effect is the increasing price of crude oil having on sales and profit margins of fuel sales in the UK?'

A quick search in Metalib gives this page, which is crammed full of downloadable data:

Energy statistics: prices

You can download annual, quarterly, monthly and weekly statistics in Microsoft Excel 2000 format from this page. You can also find more information in Energy statistics publications.

Weekly table of fuel prices
Table updated each Tuesday at 9.30 a.m.

Weekly fuel prices

Monthly tables
Rolling retail prices index UK: fuel components in the UK relative to GDP deflator (under reference QEP 2.1.1 and 2.1.2)

Retail prices index: fuels components monthly figures (QEP 2.1.3)

Typical/average annual retail prices of petroleum products and a crude oil price index (QEP 4.1.1 and 4.1.2)

Premium unleaded petrol and diesel prices in the EU (QEP 5.1.1 and 5.2.1)

Quarterly tables: 'Quarterly energy prices' (QEP)
Domestic prices
Retail prices index UK: fuel components in the UK/relative to GDP deflator (QEP 2.1.1 and 2.1.2)

Retail prices index: fuels components monthly figures (QEP 2.1.3)

Percentage of domestic electricity customers by region by supplier type (QEP 2.4.1)

Regional variation of payment method for standard electricity (QEP 2.4.2)

Regional variation of payment method for Economy 7 electricity (QEP 2.4.3)

Percentage of domestic gas customers by region by supplier type (QEP 2.5.1)

Regional variation of payment method for gas (QEP 2.5.2)

Industrial prices
Prices of fuels purchased by manufacturing industry in Great Britain (original units) (QEP 3.1.1)

Prices of fuels purchased by manufacturing industry in Great Britain (p/kWh) (QEP 3.1.2)

Average prices of fuels purchased by the major UK power producers and of gas at UK delivery points (QEP 3.2.1)

Fuel price indices for the industrial sector in current and real terms excluding/including CCL (QEP 3.3.1 and 3.3.2)

Prices of fuels purchased by non-domestic consumers in the United Kingdom excluding/including CCL (QEP 3.4.1 and 3.4.2)

Oil and petroleum product prices
Typical/average annual retail prices of petroleum products and a crude oil price index (QEP 4.1.1 and 4.1.2)

International comparisons
Premium unleaded petrol/diesel prices in the EU (QEP 5.1.1 and 5.2.1)

Industrial electricity prices in the EU for small, medium, large and extra large consumers (QEP 5.4.1, 5.4.2, 5.4.3 and 5.4.4)

Domestic electricity prices in the EU for small, medium and large consumers (QEP 5.6.1, 5.6.2 and 5.6.3)

Industrial gas prices in the EU for small, medium and large consumers (QEP 5.8.1, 5.8.2 and 5.8.3)

Domestic gas prices in the EU for small, medium and large consumers (QEP 5.10.1, 5.10.2 and 5.10.3)

Annual tables: 'Quarterly energy prices' (QEP)
Domestic prices
Retail prices index UK: fuel components in the UK relative to GDP deflator (QEP 2.1.1 and 2.1.2)

Average annual domestic electricity bills by home and non-home supplier (QEP 2.2.1)

Average annual domestic electricity bills for UK countries (QEP 2.2.2)

Average annual domestic electricity bills for selected towns and cities in the UK and average unit costs (QEP 2.2.3)

Average annual domestic gas bills by home and non-home supplier (QEP 2.3.1)

Average annual domestic gas bills for UK countries (QEP 2.3.2)

Average annual domestic gas bills for selected towns and cities in the UK and average unit costs (QEP 2.3.3)

Total household expenditure on energy in the UK (QEP 2.6.1)

Average expenditure each week on fuel per consuming household in the UK (QEP 2.6.2)

Industrial prices
Annual prices of fuels purchased by manufacturing industry (original units) (QEP 3.1.3)
Annual prices of fuels purchased by manufacturing industry (p/kWh) (QEP 3.1.4)

Oil and petroleum product prices
Typical/Average annual retail prices of petroleum products and a crude oil price index (QEP 4.1.1 and 4.1.2)
Typical retail prices of petroleum products 1970 to 2007 (QEP 4.1.3)

International comparisons
Industrial electricity prices in the EU and G7 countries (QEP 5.3.1)
Domestic electricity prices in the EU and G7 countries (QEP 5.5.1)
Industrial gas prices in the EU and G7 countries (QEP 5.7.1)
Domestic gas prices in the EU and G7 countries (QEP 5.9.1)

Annual tables: 'Digest of UK energy statistics' (DUKES)
Value balance of traded energy (DUKES 1.4–1.6)
Sales of electricity and gas by sector (DUKES 1.7)

DUKES long-term trends tables: internet only
Expenditure on energy by final user to 2008 (DUKES 1.1.6)

It is worth sitting down for a few moments and just browsing the type of material which is available through Metalib. (You may need to apply to your university librarian for an ATHENS[2] password to do this.)

The other useful source of possible data are the outline journals. For example, there are over 5,000 full-text electronic journals available via the University of Bradford library portal.

---

2   ATHENS is an Access Management System developed by Eduserv that simplifies access to the electronic resources your organization has subscribed to. Eduserv is a not-for-profit, professional IT services group.

There is also the provision of eBooks. The Library at Bradford School of Management is currently developing its eBook provision to members of the University, as are most universities. At Bradford you can view over 500 eBooks on various topics. All the available eBooks can be found via the Library Catalogue as well as a number of free eBook services (some of which need an ATHENS password to access). You will be able to find out about your own university's provision by checking with your library.

ORGANIZING YOUR DATA AND THEORIES

USING WORD OUTLINE

Word contains an outline view (look under the view section of the menu).

Outline lets you store text under ten levels of significance.

Example
1. Market Research Material
    1. Textbooks
        1. *Market Research in Practice: A guide to the basics* / Paul Hague, Nick Hague and Carol-Ann Morgan, Kogan Page, London, new edition (26 March 2004).
            1. Hague, P., Hague, N., & Morgan, C. (2004) *Market Research in Practice: A guide to the basics*, Kogan Page, London.
        2. *Marketing Research: An applied orientation* (paperback) by Naresh K. Malhotra, Pearson Education, sixth edition (11 September 2009).
            1. Malhotra, N.K. (2009) *Marketing Research: An applied orientation*, Pearson Education, London.
    2. Online Data Sources.
        1. Metalib
            1. Weekly Energy Tables (accessed 23 September 2009)
                1. http://www.decc.gov.uk/en/content/cms/statistics/source/prices/prices.aspx
                    1. stored in an Excel Table C:/data/Weeklyenergy-t1.xls

1. The data in this table suggests that the increase in price of domestic vehicle fuel is resulting in a decrease in the level of sales.

Once you have created an outline you can collapse or expand it in order in different ways.

For example:

A Level-1 view shows:

1. Market Research

A Level-2 view shows:

1. Market Research
    1. Textbooks
    2. Online Data Sources.

In this way you can view the structure of the data you are collecting at various levels of detail to help you see what you have found so far and, perhaps more importantly, see where any gaps might be.

KEEPING TRACK OF WHAT YOU FIND

There is nothing more irritating than reading a wonderful reference source and setting it aside, only to realize a few weeks later just how apt and relevant it is, how it will completely sum up your latest chain of thought – and not being able to find it again.

I have suffered from this problem many times in the past. I see a wonderful quotation – so wonderful that I know, deep in my heart, that I will never forget it. I set the book aside and then, three weeks later, I recall the quotation but have completely forgotten everything about where it is, except that it is in a book with a blue-and-yellow cover. I then spend three hours searching for the book, only to find the cover is blue and green, and then I have trawl through thirty possible index entries before I locate the quotation.

To avoid this happening to you I recommend using Post-it strips as you read a book, adding them to the page as you see interesting bits. Then, when you finish that book, turn your quotes into entries in your Word Outline, with all the detail you think you might ever need. (If you keep too much you can always delete it later; if you keep too little you are condemning yourself to many hours of searching for the original to find the missing bit – which, Sod's Law says, will always be the most vital part.)

I would suggest either using EndNote (see below) to store your bibliographical data or entering a full Harvard reference for the quotation immediately below the text as you saved it in Word Outline.

USING ENDNOTE

EndNote is a useful bibliographic tool, helping you to keep track of the books, journals and other sources that you have used to write essays.

If you enter the reference information for all the resources you use into EndNote, you can then use the program to create bibliographies for your essays, theses and dissertations, in the bibliographic style that your university requires.

Once the basic task of manually entering references has been mastered, you will be able to move on to formatting your bibliography, linking it to your Microsoft Word documents to create references in the text, and exporting and importing references from other bibliographic databases, including your University Library Catalogue.

The latest versions of EndNote available are EndNote X2 and EndNote Web.

You can find details at

http://www.bradford.ac.uk/library/elecinfo/endnote/

(You can also use an Outline level to store your Harvard References, as suggested above.)

KNOWING WHEN TO STOP SEARCHING

Once you have finished looking at (and storing in a retrievable manner) the already published information (theory or data) about your problem, you will need to decide if you have yet found sufficient material to be able to answer, with full justification, the question you have posed.

In general, only theoretical questions can be answered fully from the literature, and such questions should not really be the subject of an MBA dissertation, although they may be suitable for an MSc. It highly unlikely that published information alone will answer particular questions about the management of a unique firm in a specified set of circumstances. But it is questions of this sort which make a good MBA dissertation subject and help you, the student, to grow in understanding.

The implication of this is that you will probably need to collect additional information that is brand new. To do this you will need to look at the types of information you can collect, the means by which you can capture, store and analyse it, and the ethics of how you obtain it.

But that's another story for another chapter.

GROUP DISCUSSION TOPIC FOR CHAPTER 3

Meet in your university library and investigate the written and online sources available (asking your subject librarian is always a good idea).

Also download some typical data and experiment with Excel to see how it can be presented as graphs and charts for use in your potential dissertation.

4

DIFFERENT QUESTIONS NEED DIFFERENT ANSWERS

TAKING THE MEASURE OF AN ANSWER

I N A PREVIOUS CHAPTER I put forward a taxonomy of problems. This was:

- problems of observation;
- problems of prediction;
- problems of planning;
- problems of business theory.

I have found from the groups of students I teach that there is often some overlap between these categories, but all the problems fit within these groups. For example, out of a class of 30 MBA students 19 (63 per cent) had identified problems which fitted within a single category and 11 (37 per cent) had problems which spread over two categories. This is not a major issue, but if you find your question spans more than two areas, then it is likely that the scope of the question is going to be too wide for you to be able to complete your answer within the time and word-count limits.

When I put forward the categories of this taxonomy I selected them on the basis of how questions about each type of problem could be answered. Our next step has to be to consider how different types of question can be answered.

HOW TO ANSWER YOUR QUESTION

Each class of problem requires a different method of answering it. I intend to proceed by considering the classes of problems and then listing possible ways of providing answers.

It is important to remember that some of the most important business questions are about events or processes that will never repeat exactly. In general, the scientific approach to answering questions demands that the researcher can demonstrate repeatability. This is impossible when the subject, by its very nature, does not repeat itself. In these circumstances the best answer will create a chain of evidence which shows the logical sequence of events that caused that particular outcome. It is, however, important to bear in mind that there may well be many other logically consistent sequences which did *not* occur. Should the process be repeated, then contingency of outcome could easily lead to a result that would be quite different, but equally valid.

THE NATURE OF DATA

Whenever a problem is studied there is uncertainty about the data you collect to answer your questions about it. If your data includes forecasts, then the additional factor of uncertainty about the future is added into the mix. Because of this self-evident Truth, the only information that can be relied upon is historical information. If it cannot be measured or counted in some way, then the information is not known to be accurate. This is not to say that researchers never use information that cannot be completely verified, but you have to be prepared to distinguish between information about which there is no doubt – known as hard data – and information that is impossible to verify or repeat – known as soft data.

Hard data are any facts that can be objectively assessed. If something can be physically counted, then it is hard, objective data. Soft data are facts that can only be subjectively assessed. Any measures of opinion or attitude fall into this category, as do measures of propensity to purchase and measures of post-purchase cognitive dissonance. Hard data are amenable to statistical analysis, and most objective techniques require hard data, while the subjective methods are forced by the nature of their questions to rely upon soft data.

As far as you, as a researcher, are concerned the main difficulty when dealing with soft data is that the methods of obtaining the data must be questioned, as well as their numerical value. If a statement is made that 1,200 metres of cloth were sold last week, that statement may be easily checked by reference to either the stock records or the sales ledger. If it is also said that 85 per cent of the buyers of that cloth were satisfied with their purchase, then that statement prompts a number of questions. Who made the statement, and how reliable is his or her judgment? What is meant by the word 'satisfied'? How was this assessment arrived at, and is it really representative of all the company's customers?

Both hard and soft data are used to answer research questions, but the techniques of answering questions with them are different. The forecaster must be aware of these differences and their implications for the persuasiveness of the answers produced.

WHAT IS ACCEPTABLE ERROR IN DATA?

Something that must be considered before choosing a method of obtaining data is, How accurate does that data need to be? Achieving greater accuracy exacts two prices:

- the increased time it will take to collect large amounts of data; and
- the extra cost of collecting in-depth data of the level of accuracy needed (via individual interviews with key identified individuals, etc.).

To decide on an acceptable level of accuracy to aim for, you will have to take into account the nature of your question and what will constitute an acceptable answer. If you need only a rough indication of trends to prove your point, then an accuracy of ±100 per cent could easily be good enough. But if the answer to your question hinges on 1 or 2 per cent perturbations in the variability of the data, then obviously greater accuracy is needed. The techniques used to assess the amount of error in data collection that is allowable before it materially affects the direction of the answer are known as sensitivity analysis. Time spent in assessing the sensitivity of your answer to foreseeable errors in your data is time well spent, as it can give you a useful indication of the amount of care and effort you will need to devote to the project.

DEPENDENT AND INDEPENDENT VARIABLES

Whenever business research is undertaken, one of the fundamental questions is, What is responsible for the changes that occur? The event causing the changes is known as the dependent variable, while the outcomes it produces consist of independent variables. Independent variables change in some manner that may be predictable, but is usually outside the control of the initiator. Hence the lack of repeatability and the reliance upon contingency in any particular outcome. The dependent variables will be related in some way to the independent variables, so that when the independent variable changes it produces a change in the dependent variable. It is often difficult to identify the real independent variables in a practical situation.

To take an example, if the dependent variable is 'sales of baked beans', the independent variables could consist of the following:

- the supply of raw beans;
- the supply of tomatoes;
- the supply of sheet metal for cans;
- the capacity of the production line;
- the transport capacity of the distribution network;
- the shelf space available in supermarkets;
- the persuasiveness of the salespeople;
- the appetite of potential consumers;
- the amount of television advertising;
- the disposable income of the potential purchasers.

Any question about the sales of baked beans based on all these variables would be complex and extremely difficult to answer, as all the independent variables are dependent on other variables and would have to be studied in turn. An old folk tale, describing how to weigh a pig, aptly illustrates the difficulty.

Pigs are notoriously unco-operative when being weighed, and a method was developed to minimize the physical danger to the farmer doing the weighing. First, a long, straight plank of wood is acquired. Next, the plank is balanced exactly on top of a narrow wall. The pig is tied down on one end of the plank to prevent it from struggling, and all the participants now search around for a rock which will exactly balance the pig. (The coincidence of pig-weight and rock-weight can, of course, easily be checked by placing a spirit-level in the centre of the plank and checking that it is truly horizontal.) The search for a rock that is the exact weight of the pig may take some time, but, until a suitable rock is found, the pig will not be exactly balanced. However, once a rock *has* been found that exactly balances the pig, the rest is simple: the farmer just guesses the weight of the rock!

The moral of this is that guessing the weight of the pig in the first place would have been simpler, because it would have involved a lot less time and effort. In business research, time and effort cost money. So complications should only be introduced when they bring about either a worthwhile increase in accuracy or a substantial saving in time.

Now let's move on to the classes of problem and the means of answering questions about them.

PROBLEMS OF OBSERVATION

Problems of this sort revolve around demonstrating that the observations you have made:

- have been truly recorded;
- are an accurate representation of the subject of the observation.

To be certain that your observations have been recorded honestly, you must ensure that your recording methods are trustworthy and that the observations have been noted down to the best of your ability. The main issue here is honesty and careful attention to detail.

Accuracy of representation is a more complex issue, because it involves having some idea of what you should be seeing in order to decide if what you discovered was an accurate representation of the whole, and not simply a biased or bigoted selection from it. Fortunately, when dealing with large samples, statistical methods can be helpful. The theory of statistics has revealed that large populations have predictable ranges of possibilities. However, with most research problems you will have to restrict your investigations to a relatively small sample of the population you are studying. In order to check that your sample is a reasonable representation of the population of interest, you need to compare its characteristics to the theoretical models that you intend to use to describe its variability. For example, if you plan to model your population, assuming the thing you are measuring is normally distributed, then you must show the distribution to be Normal and not of some other form, such as Binomial or Poisson. You may also need to use extrapolation from your sampling model to work out the expected range of error you are encountering, to see if it is acceptable.

PROBLEMS OF PREDICTION

The issues here involve demonstrating that the basis for prediction

- is founded on past behaviour patterns;
- would have worked if applied to past events;
- and so offers a reasonable possibility of working when applied to the future.

BASED ON PAST BEHAVIOUR PATTERNS

To make the best use of historical data you need to have some understanding of the underlying patterns that may be present in it. All objective techniques make some assumptions about the patterns present in the historical information, but applying a technique that assumes one type of pattern to a data set that exhibits a different pattern can cause wildly inaccurate results. Three basic patterns may be present in historical data (and they may be combined to produce the more complex patterns needed to explain complicated data).

Horizontal or stationary patterns

These are data patterns that are not changing. Hence, if we consider time as the independent variable, the data, when plotted, appear as a horizontal line. This type of pattern is often referred to as a stationary time series. In reality, the data will never show a totally straight line, because there will be variations, both above and below the stationary line. In a true stationary series the sum of all the positive excursions will be equal to the sum of the negative excursions, so the forecast takes the form of some variant of the equation:

$$forecast\ value = average\ value + error$$

Horizontal patterns appear very often in short-term forecasting, because any data will approximate to a stationary series if the time interval for the forecast is short enough. Many of the simpler forecasting techniques assume that the underlying pattern of the response is a horizontal straight line.

Trend patterns

A trend data pattern consists of a straight line which shows either an upward or a downward slope. Whereas the horizontal pattern was entirely described by its average value, the trend pattern needs two parameters to define it. These two parameters are the gradient of the line and the intercept. The basic form of the trend forecast equation is:

$$forecast\ value = gradient \times independent\ variable + intercept + error$$

Any business which is either growing or declining will exhibit trend patterns in its sales data, and an accurate assessment of the slope of the trend, as well as any changes in the direction of the trend, are vital to the smooth running of the business.

Seasonal patterns

A seasonal data pattern repeats itself in a regular manner, creating a repetitive pattern which has a predictable recurrence throughout a time period. The mathematical function that describes the variation of the data in a periodic manner is called a time-dependent function. All the techniques that assume a seasonal data pattern make use of methods which seek to determine the nature of the time-dependent function. The important describing parameters of the time-dependent function are its periodicity and its amplitude. The periodicity is the length of time between two adjacent peaks or troughs, while the amplitude is the distance from peak to trough. Any data pattern with a period of more than twelve months is referred to as a cyclical. Cyclical or seasonal data patterns are described by an equation of the form shown below:

forecast value = f (time) × independent variable + error

A typical example of a product with a seasonal sales pattern is the lawn-mower. Lawn-mowers are mainly sold in the spring and summer – when grass is growing, and people need something to cut their grass – with very few sales during the autumn and winter. When considering whether sales data are seasonal, we must bear in mind that a season does not always have to be twelve months long; it could well be shorter.

Long-term cyclical effects are often observed in situations that involve natural reproductive processes. An example is the price of beef, which has an approximate five-year cycle, due to the time it takes to build up a sizeable herd after it has been allowed to run down. Another example is the sales of towelling nappies for babies. Nappy sales are affected by the birth rate, and this exhibits a cyclical trend; sixteen years or more after children are born they become part of the breeding population.

In practice it is rare to find data patterns that conform exactly to the patterns just described. The main exception is the horizontal type, which can often be used as a first approximation to any of the others, provided the time period being considered is brief enough. To try to model the more complex patterns encountered in business life, the three basic patterns have to be combined in order to find a suitable explanation of the behaviour of the data. It is thus quite possible that a model for a particular set of data could consist of a trend upon which both seasonal and cyclical variations have been superimposed.

Did it fit past events?

Before attempting to use any forecasting technique it is essential to know what data pattern is assumed by the model used in the technique. If the proposed method is to stand any chance of successfully forecasting the future, then it must fit the historical data to hand. (The only exception to this rule of thumb is when the forecaster suspects that the market has undergone a complete change in its underlying structure which completely negates all past experience.)

The question facing the researcher is how to identify the existence of any patterns in the historical data that have been collected. Various complex computer algorithms exist for the automatic recognition of patterns. However, the human brain is remarkably well adapted for such pattern recognition, provided the data are presented in the right way. The easiest way to spot patterns is to plot the data on a graph and simply to look for the basic patterns described above. The experienced human eye and brain can easily spot patterns that are disguised by random fluctuations unconnected with the underlying trends of the data.

The choice of scale for the vertical (dependent) axis of the graph is important, because too cramped a scale will turn all data into stationary patterns. Conversely, too extended a scale will prevent you from seeing the range and variation of the data. The choice of scale for the horizontal (independent) axis is also important, so that any long-period cyclical patterns can be observed (it must not be forgotten that in the very short term almost any data will approximate to a horizontal pattern). To some extent the time scale of the graph will be dictated by the aggregation of the raw data: if sales figures have been collected at monthly intervals, any weekly seasonality cannot be detected. Similarly, unless at least 120 months' data are available, there is little opportunity of detecting a five-yearly cyclical pattern.

Can it reliably estimate future developments?

To satisfy this criterion, all you need to do is collect sufficient data to be able to ignore and not use the latest points. You can then apply your chosen technique to the earlier data and see if it predicts what actually happened. If it doesn't, then your method doesn't work.

PROBLEMS OF PLANNING

SHOWING THE PLAN IS APPROPRIATE

Demonstrating the appropriateness of a plan will involve observing and recording the circumstances of the organization you are studying; creating a proposed method of transforming it to the new desired state; and, finally, showing by a listing of episodic evidence that the plan both agrees with the known attributes of the organization and also offers a logical series of steps from the existing state to the new state. Clearly, this type of problem is a two-stage one, the first step encompassing all the problems of observation already discussed, plus the additional need to develop and demonstrate the robustness of the plan based on the observations.

SHOWING HOW THE PLAN CAN AMELIORATE THE PROBLEM

To demonstrate the results of a plan before it is implemented entails making a logical case to show how the organization will be improved. Having shown the plan to be appropriate, as outlined above, you then need to carry out the additional process of predicting the outcome of implementation. This will involve predicting what changes the plan will cause. You first need to solve the observational problem of describing the existing status of the organization. Then you must develop your plan and show it to be logical and reasonable. Next you need to predict the post-plan status of the organization, within the confines of the scenario defined by the plan, and finally to compare the predicted status with the existing status and draw a comparison between the two.

SHOWING HOW IMPLEMENTING THE PLAN WORKED AS PREDICTED

Each of the types of planning problem has required answers of increasing complexity. This final type requires all the steps of the previous two, plus a period of recorded active intervention, followed by a second period of observation (with its associated problems) to determine the result. Finally, you will have to compare the goodness of fit between the observations and the predictions using statistical techniques (chi-square, correlation, etc.). Problems of this type yield powerful questions and compelling answers, but take a lot of time and effort to do well.

PROBLEMS OF BUSINESS THEORY

DEVELOPING A NEW THEORY FROM SCRATCH

This is not a suitable topic for an MBA, MA or MSc dissertation. It would be more suited for a PhD project.

SHOWING HOW AN EXISTING THEORY CAN BE ADAPTED TO A NEW SITUATION

This type of problem is essentially a mixture of observation, prediction and planning. Having observed the organization, the next step is to show where the existing theory fails to explain the new observations. Then the theory must be adjusted, within the restraints of its assumptions, to see if the mismatches can be explained; this is essentially a planning problem. If the theory can be adapted, the next step is to predict how the modified theory can be used to explain the new circumstances. Finally, the predictions of the modified theory must be compared to actual circumstances (a problem of observation), and either the modifications accepted or a new cycle of modification started.

TESTING IF AN EXISTING THEORY REMAINS APPLICABLE IN NEW CIRCUMSTANCES

This is essentially a combination of prediction and observation problems. The circumstances of the organization must first be observed, the predicted values of the theory calculated, and finally a comparison made between theory and practice. It will probably be necessary to use statistical methods to determine how good the fit is between theory and practice.

SOURCES OF DATA

HOW TO FIND APPROPRIATE DATA

The availability of data is of central importance to any postgraduate business project. Depending upon the degree of accuracy required, the solution to most problems requires that a considerable amount of data be collected and analysed. For example, it would be no good trying to answer a question about long historical time sequences if data were only available for the past two months. Similarly, using a complex econometric technique with many variables would be fruitless when the necessary data are not available. Furthermore, if the validity and/or accuracy of your source data are questionable, it would be neither worthwhile nor cost-effective to spend time and effort on a sophisticated analysis.

In data analysis, the principle of 'rubbish in, rubbish out' applies: your results will only be as good as the data you have collected. The quality of your basic data is critical. No matter how sophisticated your analysis, if the basic data are poor, the results will be at best of limited use, and at worst worthless.

You might conclude that all this is obvious, but they are facts that I cannot emphasize enough. If you start with incorrect or poor data, then no matter how skilfully you manipulate it, it is still going to yield poor results. Like a good dwelling, a good dissertation is built on solid foundations – and that means good data. It is the preparation at the beginning that achieves the professional finish.

You will recall that when I first introduced this topic I asked you to consider possible problems and questions. I also asked you to consider what data you would need to be able to answer your question. Now I intend to consider where you get the necessary data.

There is no hard and fast rule for this, and what the most promising sources are will depend on your choice of problem and question. Generally speaking, there are two main categories of existing sources of data you might be able to use:

- Internal data, generated within a company – such as future company plans, sales statistics and other internal records. For certain situations this may be sufficient, if you are simply interested in general or cyclical trends that can be projected to answer a prediction question.

- Secondary data, generated outside the company – such as government and trade statistics and published marketing research surveys. These external sources can cover sales for the industry as a whole, income, population trends, etc., and bear some relationship to the sales of the company.

Both are important, and in many research situations it is necessary to use both sources to a greater or lesser degree.

A third category of data are those collected specifically for the research task – through some form of marketing research technique, such as a sample survey or a test market, or through observational studies. This is termed primary data, and it is usually the most time-consuming to obtain. Before embarking on such an exercise, you should undertake a full exploratory investigation of existing data sources, both internal and external, to see whether the data are already available elsewhere. Why re-invent the wheel by generating primary data when existing secondary data sources can provide the data in a fraction of the time for a fraction of the effort?

Most of the above refers to statistical sources that can be analysed in order to formulate quantitative judgments. Such research methods are termed objective. But qualitative judgments also have a place. Factors such as marketing plans and strategies, together with the likely activity of competitors, might have to be taken into consideration. Such research is a more individualistic matter, and the techniques used are called subjective methods. When writing an MBA dissertation, subjective judgments can be quantified in some way in order to make them more objective.

INTERNAL DATA FROM YOUR ORGANIZATION

For any organization to function efficiently and effectively, it is necessary to generate information. Some people, quite understandably, feel too much emphasis is placed on form-filling and record-keeping, and most employees regard the internal bureaucracy of the organization as, at best, a time-consuming but necessary evil. To an MBA researcher, though, internal documentation and records are a treasure trove of potentially useful information.

For many observation and prediction problems, some sort of past and current organizational statistics are needed, if only to benchmark the present or provide a base for extrapolation into the future. And there will be aspects of many problems that can only be elucidated by a detailed look at the organization's own data.

Desk research into internal company records is most useful. It is a logical starting point for collecting data in many research exercises. One advantage of such information is that the departmental manager concerned can usually give an indication of how appropriate it is to the research problem and provide an opinion on its accuracy. One disadvantage is that, although the organization's internal system may include useful information, it may be difficult for the researcher to obtain it in an appropriate form, either because of the inflexibility of the system or because of indifference and lack of co-operation by individual departments.

A researcher with little idea of what is happening in his or her own firm has very little prospect of producing sensible answers to their questions. Successfully obtaining past data from within the organization will depend to a great extent on knowing the firm and its staff well, so the first stage in seeking data is to take a 'systems-analysis' approach and carefully follow through the firm's documentary procedures. A great deal of information can be obtained by merely talking to heads of departments and staff involved in the data-collection procedures. Getting access to information and files may at times be problematic, in that some departments will willingly co-operate while others may be indifferent or simply 'too busy'. Hence building up friendly relationships to obtain co-operation is important. Failing this, it may be necessary to carry out a formal full information audit, authorized by top management, requesting that heads of departments provide positive assistance.

The researcher should look carefully at how data are obtained, altered, processed and circulated throughout the organization and what records are kept. Every document should be noted, possibly using some form of flow-chart. The type of documentation and the function it serves should be recorded, as well as its origin and destination. Administrative and documentary procedures will vary from company to company, but most commercial systems will start with a customer's inquiry and end with billing that customer. With analysis, it will be possible to identify the main steps in the procedure of each department. The idea is to build up a picture of the system from individual employees' methods up to the total departmental system, and ultimately to that of the organization as a whole.

Many records are kept by individual members of staff on an 'unofficial' basis – perhaps in case a question is asked about something, or for some other contingency. These unofficial sources may be very useful to the researcher, and can only be identified through careful probing. In practice, it is often surprising to discover exactly what information is kept and maintained for personal use in this manner.

Now I will try to provide examples of the types of internal information that may be useful to you as a researcher. The list is not exhaustive, and your actual information requirements will depend on your choice of problem and the nature of your question.

INTERNAL DATA FROM A MARKETING DEPARTMENT

The marketing department is the main point of commercial interaction between a firm and its customers. Consequently, a great deal of information should be available, including the following.

Sales volume by product and product group

This information can be aggregated into total sales volume, but it also allows you to evaluate the contribution to the total volume made by each type of product or product line.

Sales volume by area

This may be in terms of sales territories or other geographical areas (e.g. East Midlands, North Yorkshire, etc.) or by standard media areas, as used by the Joint Industry Committee for Television Advertising Research (JICTAR) or other similar surveys.

Sales volume by market segment

The basis for segmentation may be regional, or – in the case of, say, an industrial market – by type of industry (e.g. a firm may supply steel castings to both the pump and valve industries). Such information will give an indication of which segments are likely to remain static, which are declining, and which show growth possibilities for the future. Where the firm deals with a few large customers, segmentation may be by type of customer, and any change in demand from either individuals or types may be highly significant in terms of forecasting sales and materials requirements.

Sales volume by type of distribution channel

Where a company has a multi-channel distribution policy, it is possible to calculate the effectiveness and profitability of each type of channel. This also allows identification of trends in the pattern of distribution, which in turn can be taken into account in forecasting future channel requirements. Channel information by geographical area may show a difference in the profitability of one type of channel in different parts of the country, allowing for profitable geographical channel differentiation. To contribute to a more realistic forecast, information can be gathered by type of selling outlet (multiples, wholesalers, agents, factors, etc.). Such information allows researchers to identify and develop promising channel opportunities, resulting in more effective channel marketing.

Sales volume over time

In terms of actual sales and units sold, this measure allows any seasonal variation to be identified. Inflation and price adjustments can also be taken into consideration.

Pricing information

This includes historical information relating to price adjustments by product and allows the researcher to establish the effect on demand of price increases or decreases and to judge the likely effects of future price changes.

Communication mix information

Here past data on the effects of advertising campaigns, sponsorship or direct-mail programmes or exhibitions are analysed. Levels of expenditure on marketing communications, and the effect on sales of increasing or decreasing such expenditure are noted. Again, such information will act as a guide as to the effectiveness of future communication expenditure plans.

Sales promotion data

These provide information on the effectiveness of past promotion campaigns (e.g. reduced-price packs, coupons, self-liquidating offers or competitions aimed at customers). Also included are trade incentives – aimed at the trade, including distributors, multiples, wholesalers and retailers. The impact of incentive schemes for in-house company personnel can also be analysed in terms of changes in level of sales.

Sales representatives' records and reports

Many sales representatives keep a customer file on every 'live' customer. Often such records include considerable detail, ranging from information on individual customer interests and hobbies, number of children and other personal information to information about the customer's firm, its product range, diversification plans and likely future purchases. Even information on what the customer said to the salesman on the last visit is likely to be recorded. In some industries such data is held on a Customer Relationship Management System, which can be used to create reports. In addition, sales representatives often send reports to the sales office on such matters as orders lost to competitors (and possible reasons why), firms that are holding future purchasing decisions in abeyance for one reason or another, or firms that have received quotations but are no longer interested. All such information can be useful to the forecaster as background 'intelligence' information.

Inquiries received and quotations dispatched

Customers normally submit a written inquiry asking for details of prices, delivery, etc., probably doing the same to a number of potential suppliers. Inquiries often lead to detailed quotations, which are submitted to the potential customer. This information may be useful to the researcher, who may be able to establish patterns both in the percentage of inquiries that mature into purchase orders, and in the average length of time between a quotation being submitted and an order being received. The number of requests for quotations can provide a guide to economic activity in the market place, and – because firms are likely to request quotations from a number of potential suppliers – those successfully converted into orders can give an indication of the company's share of the total market.

INTERNAL DATA FROM OTHER DEPARTMENTS

Finance Department

The management accountant will be able to provide accurate cost data on areas of interest as well as other useful material like past management reports, which might give information on such matters as rates of absenteeism among production staff. This could give the researcher useful pointers. Management information requirements differ from firm to firm, but these reports may contain accurate information on things like the number of new customers in a given period, number of withdrawals, numbers of items sold by product in volume and monetary terms, total sales by sales personnel area, division, etc. In addition, past budgets, complete with variance analyses showing budgeted figures against actual figures, will be kept for all departments within the organization, and again this can be a valuable source of accurate historical information.

The Finance Department will also keep statistics on current operations, such as orders received, orders dispatched and orders in hand. This data is kept for internal management information needs and also out of the legal necessity to gather information in order to present the accounts for auditing purposes. Such information will duplicate information held elsewhere, but it may be more accessible via the Finance Department. In addition, because financial information has to some extent been collected independently, it can be used as a check against other departmental data to ensure that no important information has been overlooked or misinterpreted.

Purchasing Department

Information that may be of use here includes copies of old purchase orders, materials lists, requisitions, materials status schedule reports, and information on suppliers, such as reliability of delivery, lead times and price lists. The department will also be able to provide stock-control data relating to re-order levels, buffer and safety stock levels, economic order quantities and stock turn by inventory item. The forecaster may need to take such information into account because stock availability and short lead times may be part of the general level of service offered by the firm to customers. Depending on the service sensitivity of the market, service levels could have a very significant influence on demand. A good example is provided by the North Sea oil industry service companies, where price is of less importance but service is paramount. A company with a service level marginally higher than that of competitors could gain a competitive advantage. Obviously, present and future service levels will have a bearing on both sales and materials management, because an increase in the level of service will mean more stock and a greater variety of materials being held. This will naturally lead to higher levels of working capital being needed to finance these stocks, but it may be necessary in order to provide the levels of service required in the industry.

Transport Department

The Transport or Dispatch Department will have its own information system, cataloguing in chronological order details of goods dispatched, method of transportation (i.e. own vehicle or outside contractor), the weight of goods dispatched and copies of advice notes and other delivery documents. Again, such information may be useful in its own right or may act as a means of checking similar information gathered from other departments.

Production Department

The Production Department should be able to supply documentation relating to production control. It will keep copies of works orders, materials lists and design information. These could provide information on orders placed in the firm's own workshops, requisitions for materials to stores, orders subcontracted to other suppliers, manufacturing times, machine utilization times and order completion dates. Such information will probably be available elsewhere in the organization, but may be more easily obtainable from this source. It may supplement existing sources or act as a cross-check on information from other departments.

USING DEPARTMENTAL PLANS

Past and current internal information may be available to the researcher, but so are the short-, medium- and long-term plans of the company relating to individual departments.

Naturally, future planned activity and changes in company policy or methods of operation could have a considerable bearing on prediction and planning problems, and such factors need to be taken into account. You need to answer a number of questions like: Does the Sales Department have plans to expand the sales force? Does Marketing plan to increase advertising and other promotional expenditure? Does the company intend to invest in capital equipment – more efficient machine tools in the Production Department, or a new materials-handling system for the warehouse? Are HR planning to take on more staff? Likely future events such as these may significantly affect future performance.

The sources I've just discussed are examples of the type of internal information available to researchers. Other departments such as Personnel, Research & Development, Work Study, Organization & Methods, etc., may also hold useful information. Which departments you approach for information will tend to depend on the nature of your problem and questions.

EXTERNAL SECONDARY DATA

It is important for researchers to have at their disposal as much relevant information as possible, within the constraints of time and word count. At times data generated within the firm may be sufficient for their needs. However, variables outside the firm, in the general business and economic environment, will often also have a bearing on the situation. Therefore, for some types of question, internally generated data may need to be interpreted in the light of information relating to past, present and likely future external factors, trends and events.

For other types of questions, external data will be by far the most important source – for example, when a researcher is trying to predict total industry sales using government-published statistics on production and productivity. At other times external data may merely augment internal information.

External sources of data include statistics and reports issued by governments, trade associations and other, mainly private, organizations. Advertising agencies and research companies often circulate useful information. National newspapers, trade journals and directories are also a fruitful source of relevant information. Most of these sources can be found in any good university library, and some bigger cities may have a dedicated reference library. Any information reference that is required but cannot be found on the library shelves is usually available through the inter-library loan service, or from the British Library itself, or accessed via the ATHENS system.

External published secondary data can be placed in two categories:

- data on the general economy and the outside business environment;
- industry- or market-specific data which may relate to certain products or product lines, or may be more general in nature.

GOVERNMENT STATISTICS

The Government Statistical Service comprises the statistics divisions of all major government departments in addition to the government's own collecting agencies – the Business Statistics Office, the Office of Population Censuses and Surveys, and the Central Statistical Office (which co-ordinates the whole collection process). The publications of government departments are too extensive to list here, so I shall only mention the more important ones.

Government Statistics, a brief guide to sources. Free from the Central Statistical Office, CO:CSO Section, Great George Street, London SW1P 3AQ. An annual publication.

List of Principal Statistical Series and Publications. This is No. 20 in 'Studies in Official Statistics' series published by Her Majesty's Stationery Office (HMSO).

Business Monitors can give facts about your industry. Free from the Central Statistical Office.

Guide to Official Statistics. An annual publication from the Central Statistical Office.

Government Publications. A monthly publication from The Stationery Office, Atlantic House, Holborn Viaduct, London EC1P 1BN.

Two further useful addresses:

Statistics and Market Intelligence Library, 50 Ludgate Hill, London EC4M 7HU.

Government Bookshop, 48 High Holborn, London WC1V 6HB.

NON-GOVERNMENT STATISTICS

There are also many non-government sources of information, ranging from trade association reports to the business pages of national newspapers. Many of these can be accessed via Metalib.

You should remember that all external secondary data were once primary data collected for a particular reason. It is often the case, particularly with government sources, that assumptions and conventions have been used in their collection and analysis. If you use these data it is important that you are aware of the assumptions and conventions used so that you can take them into account when assessing data accuracy, or can make necessary adjustments. If you don't do this, there is a danger of producing data you think are accurate because you have assumed the original data were themselves accurate, when, in the context in which you have used them, they are not. If a major decision is to be based upon such a piece of research, it could be a costly (and career-limiting) mistake.

DATA FROM ORIGINAL RESEARCH

Up to now we have looked at collecting of data that already exist – either information from within an organization, or from external sources. When these types of data source have been investigated and evaluated, you may still find you do not yet have enough information of the appropriate type, and you have an 'information gap' to fill. Often, secondary data will not provide a complete solution to a research problem. Therefore they need to be augmented by primary data. (Primary data, in this context, are data collected specifically for your research task: i.e. original data.)

Whether or not you need to collect original data will depend on the nature of the problem and the detail of the question you asked. For some problems and questions you may need to generate your own primary data. Existing secondary data may not be obtainable, or may be incomplete or unreliable – or it may have been collected for an entirely different purpose. In the last case the data may have been tabulated and published in such a way that a great deal of data processing is needed to convert it into a form that can be used to answer your question. In that process a significant amount of the original accuracy may be lost, which may reduce the level of confidence that can be placed in the final result. Moreover, doing the processing correctly could take a lot of time and expertise, and you might run out of time, or off the end of your word count, before you complete the task.

It may be that data are somewhat obsolete by the time they are published, and market conditions, the position and actions of competitors or other factors may have radically changed. It may also be that the subject of your questions is a new product concept, and existing data are simply not available. In such a situation the generation of primary data through test marketing and other research techniques may be your only possible source. How might you do it?

USING MARKETING RESEARCH TO GATHER PRIMARY DATA

There are numerous types of field research and areas of investigation that can be used to gather primary information. Which to use will clearly depend upon your choice of problem and questions. I have outlined some significant ones below.

Market

This includes assessing the market size and competition in existing and new markets; market structure and segmentation studies; measuring market potentials; market share analysis; determining market characteristics; short-, medium- and long-term market trend analysis; investigating whether the market is declining, static or growing; locating potential customers geographically; finding out customers' age, sex, occupation and social status; and identifying the economic and other environmental trends affecting the market.

Packaging

This includes research into the visual impact of packs at the point of sale; package label evaluation; the brand image of the product conveyed by the pack; and the effect of different pack sizes, shapes and colours on sales.

Sales

This involves examining the firm's selling activities and the effectiveness of its sales force and sales-force incentive schemes; and determining territorial variations in sales yield; looking at methods of operation, sales call planning, remuneration, supervision and sales training; comparing company sales with total industry sales; determining whether or not the company's sales are expanding at the same rate as the market as a whole, and whether sales are seasonal, constant or cyclical.

Communications

This includes evaluating advertising effectiveness – both pre-testing and post-testing viewer response to offerings, copy-comprehension testing, copy testing, media research, readership, viewership and listener-ship studies; and evaluating other elements in the communications mix, such as exhibitions, sponsorship, trade journals, direct mail, sales promotions and public relations.

Pricing

This includes studies of price awareness and price sensitivity of the market and market segments; comparing the effect on consumer price/value perceptions of different product formulations, packaging and communication mixes; examining the effectiveness of price reductions as promotional tools; and assessing consumer and trade perceptions of price in relation to competitive prices and the likely effects of price changes on demand.

Customer

This covers psychological investigations into consumers' purchasing motivations and their attitudes towards products, which can be done through investigations into buyer behaviour at both trade and user levels. Reasons for customer preferences for certain colours, brands and sizes can be researched, together with their perceived images of the company in terms of quality, delivery, reliability and service.

Comparing attitudes towards the company and its products in relation to competitive offerings is an area where field research can yield important information, because such qualitative information is unlikely to be available from existing sources and could well have a bearing on the answer to your question.

Distribution

This includes studying retail distribution and retail behaviour; the effectiveness of the total distribution system; the level of service the organization's distribution system offers compared with competition; the service sensitivity of the market. It also includes identifying the service elements important to customers, and establishing how service requirements are being met. These will be effective indicators of company performance, and an evaluation of customer reaction to changes in service levels will be an important contribution to the final forecast.

Product

This includes analysing the competitive strengths and weaknesses of the organization's products in relation to competing products; investigating new uses and markets for existing products; and looking at new product development, idea generation, concept testing, business analysis and test marketing. Such information is needed if your questions concern a prediction of likely sales.

Other specialist areas

These specifically include: industrial marketing research; plant, retail and warehouse location studies; export and international studies; and business and economic studies.

This list is incomplete, but it does indicate the scope of research activities. A fuller listing of the techniques and their detailed workings can be obtained from any good marketing research textbook.

HOW TO COLLECT PRIMARY DATA

OBSERVATION

This research technique has many applications in gathering data for forecasting. It may be used on its own or in conjunction with other methods. Very often information from one type of research method needs to be supplemented by observation for the researcher to gain a complete picture. For example, answers to some questions during a personal interview may be thought by the respondent to be too trivial to remember, but such information may be of particular importance to the researcher. In a retail study, one may wish to know how the respondent moved around a supermarket, which stands were visited first, whether the promotional stand was looked at and whether a promotional leaflet was taken or not. Studies such as store traffic flows can only be carried out by observation. The main methods of such experimental observations are these.

Mechanical or electronic devices

A simple example of this method of observation is recording traffic passing a certain location. This is often done for road transport studies, but in a marketing research context it may be carried out for poster site research. Similar traffic counts are carried out in stores for 'flow' studies. Where permitted, unseen devices – such as one-way mirrors, hidden cameras or MP3 recorders – are highly effective for observing and recording uninhibited customer behaviour. Devices such as the tachistoscope (for measuring rates of recognition), the eye camera (for charting eye movements) and psychogalvanometers (for measuring arousal to certain stimuli) are often used in laboratory conditions to pre-test advertisements. In some instances respondents are aware of such recording devices – the special monitoring devices on television sets to record viewing habits are an example.

The audit technique

This is widely used for market size information, distribution data, trend data and brand-share data. The retail audit carried out by Nielsen is a good example of this technique. It is also the reason why many supermarkets issue loyalty cards, which link audit data to individual consumers.

Physical checks of opening stocks, deliveries between visits and closing stocks are undertaken as well as electronic data capture of actual sales. The number of brands recorded in summary reports that are subsequently purchased by clients depends on their individual requirements. As well as estimating overall consumer sales, the retail audit monitors other aspects such as merchandizing and selling programmes associated with brands in the particular product field. A similar technique is the domestic consumer panel operated by such organizations as Audits of Great Britain. A panel records details of consumer purchases and gives information about the characteristics of those who buy, together with their purchasing habits. This can be done by a company carrying out a 'pantry audit' or a 'dustbin audit'. The pantry audit involves a visit to check on the respondent's larder shelves, while the dustbin audit entails the subject placing empty packets, cans, etc., into specially provided receptacles that are collected regularly. These are then counted to derive information on usership rates, brand loyalty, etc. In the case of fast-moving consumer goods, purchasers are sometimes asked to record the data in a specially designed diary suitably coded for computer analysis. Fast-moving items are usually counted on a weekly basis, but panel data on consumer durables may be based on a longer-term collection and count basis. In addition, many retailers run their own loyalty card schemes to link customers' names and addresses to the purchase data captured by electronic point-of-sale tills.

Human observation

A simple method here is to use merchandizing staff, who can be trained to observe customers' behaviour while they are shopping. Customers can be monitored to see whether they look at special displays or read the details of promotional literature as they move around the store. In general, observation gives information about what people do, but not about why they do it. Therefore, after respondents have been observed, they may be approached and asked to answer questions or complete a questionnaire.

EXPERIMENT

Another method of obtaining primary data for research is through marketing experiments. These are methods of organizing the collection of evidence so that hypotheses may be tested.

The theoretical aspects associated with experimental design are detailed, and at times complex. Specialist texts on marketing research and statistics cover such technicalities in depth, so I shall only give an outline here, to illustrate the sorts of situation in which experimentation can usefully help in collecting research data.

In scientifically controlled experiments the rule is to hold all variables constant except the variable to be studied and measured. Changes in the test situation are examined for statistical significance, and, if they are significant, this is attributed to the influence of the independent variable. This could be applied to a marketing experiment whose object may be to compare responses to several possible alternatives in the company's marketing mix.

Perhaps the most common form of experimental marketing is test marketing a new or improved product. The technique involves selecting some geographical area that is purportedly representative of the eventual total market (a 'microcosm of the universe') and launching the new product or brand in this area under conditions as nearly as possible identical to those that would apply in a national launch. Marketing support – advertising, promotion, merchandizing and personal selling, etc. – are also, as far as possible, representative of those of a national launch. The duration of the test will depend on the repurchase cycle and the time it takes to reach a predefined level of market penetration. Information from such experiments allows the researcher to predict the likely performance of the product in a national launch.

Experiments can also be used to test the effects of changes in marketing mix variables on the sales of existing products . Experimentation is the only research method available for actually verifying cause-and-effect relationships in marketing studies. Examples of experimental situations are:

- variations in sales-force efficiency resulting from different types of sales training;
- variations in sales as a result of different combinations of display width, shelf height and shelf fullness in a supermarket;
- to establish what combination of merchandising, coupon offer and price reduction is most effective, and the degree of interaction, if any, between the variables;
- variations in sales due to different pack sizes, colours and tastes of the product.

Advertising experiments can be planned using 'split runs' and changing either the amount of advertising or the type of advertisement in alternative editions (or sometimes within the same edition) of a publication, and monitoring the response to different formats. This can be achieved by measuring the different response rates to a promotional offer when coupled with the advertisement in one format as against the advertisement in a different format.

The object of experimentation is to ascertain the amount of variation in, say, sales that can be attributed to the variable or treatment under study, and what amount of variance is attributable to other factors or merely to chance.

Experimental designs range from the relatively simple, such as 'time series analysis': where, for example, sales are monitored for a period of time before some change in the marketing mix and then after it, to see what happens to the time series as a result. More complex experiments involve multivariable designs – such as the 'Latin square' experiment, or – if interaction is present – a 'factorial design' format can be used to isolate the effects of variation and interaction of more than one variable at a time. The forms of these experiments are adequately detailed in any good marketing research textbook, if you find your problem requires you to use them.

SURVEYS

A sample survey is probably the most familiar method of collecting primary data. Survey methodology, such as sampling and question-naire design, must be carried out correctly if any confidence is to be placed in the data. The detailed methodology is covered in depth in a number of marketing research texts.

A sample survey is a technique to elicit information from other people, who may be agents, distributors, suppliers or customers. Some companies carry out their own survey work, but it is more usual for firms to commission such work from professional agencies. Examples that are quite familiar are public opinion surveys conducted by firms such as Audits of Great Britain, the British Market Research Bureau, and Gallup. Some of the larger agencies offer a very comprehensive range of marketing research services. Gallup, for example, carry out field research ranging from political and social surveys to areas such as leisure, travel, catering, staff recruitment and labour relations. Other research agencies are more specialized, such as Food and Drink Research Ltd. For the type of small-scale surveys carried out as part of an MBA research project, you will usually carry out your own interviews, although sometimes organizations do allow students to subcontract surveys. Such commissioned surveys should be treated as secondary data when writing up.

Survey methods can be used to gather information on a wide range of topics. Similarly, surveys can be used to gather information for sales-forecasting purposes, if your problem is one of prediction. You can, for example, survey the probable consumer reaction to a product, pack or price modification, or the purchasing plans of professional buyers in a particular industrial market segment.

The research instrument used in most survey work is the questionnaire. Careful planning should go into the design of the questionnaire, so that the questions asked are meaningful and unambiguous to respondents, and the information gained is useful and achieves the objectives of your survey.

METHODS OF INQUIRY

Postal surveys

Questionnaires are sent to respondents through the post for completion and return. This is a relatively inexpensive method of surveying a sample of the population, its main disadvantage being that respondent rates are often low. Non-response may be a source of bias, as non-respondents may be significantly different in some way from respondents.

Telephone surveys

This is similar to the postal questionnaire, except that the questionnaire is read out by the interviewer to the respondent over the telephone. This method is used more frequently in industrial survey work. In a telephone interview there is no opportunity to show the respondent supporting material, such as attitude scales or multi-choice answer cards, which in case of the personal interview can help to sustain interest and increase understanding. So telephone interviewing works well when the questions to be asked are fairly straightforward; in more detailed business inquiries the telephone interview will often precede a personal interview. The initial telephone call may be used to select subjects for a personal interview.

Personal interview surveys

Here the questionnaire is administered by the researcher to a selected sample of the population. If the questionnaire is long, or the questions complicated, the best results can be obtained through a personal interview. Interviewers often work to a quota sample, interviewing numbers of people from specific social classes according to a scheme predetermined at the sampling centre; the researcher uses his/her judgment as to which respondents to choose, and when the quota is reached, the survey is complete. When interviewing, you should be aware of the importance of such matters as avoiding bias when asking questions, the correct interviewing manner, etc. (these topics are covered in good market research textbooks).

Focus groups and depth interviews

These are valuable techniques for obtaining primary data. They are often used in the 'exploratory stage' of the research process, when you have little knowledge about the precise nature of the problem, and so do not yet have the information needed for a full field survey exercise. They allow a researcher to explore a situation by consulting people concerned with the research problem. These may be customers, users, distributors, agents, experts, sales and technical staff or other company personnel. Basically, the techniques involve encouraging a limited number of people to talk freely and at length about their behaviour, needs and wants, and motivations. If sales and technical staff are being interviewed, they may be asked questions on what they really feel about the company and its products, the competition and their experience in the field.

Group discussions and depth interviews are the two most used methods in qualitative research. Respondents are either contacted individually or brought together in groups of about eight to ten (a number small enough to encourage general discussion and large enough to make it likely that group members will have a variety of ideas).

The point of group discussions and depth interviews is to probe deep beneath the surface to find out what the respondents really think, so the data obtained are usually qualitative. The techniques are based on small samples which are not substantial enough to be able to draw statistical conclusions. It is possible to conduct enough lengthy, unstructured interviews to draw statistical conclusions, and this is sometimes done, but it is costly in terms of time and commitment. However, these techniques are usually for exploratory purposes, to obtain enough data to design a quantitative study of a sample large enough to allow conclusions to be drawn.

GROUP DISCUSSION TOPIC FOR CHAPTER 4

Return to your written assignment for Chapter 1 and identify what type of answer your question requires and then discuss exactly how you would collect appropriate data.

Take notes on the discussion to add to your Learning Log.

5

HOW TO USE STATISTICS

RUMMAGING IN THE STATISTICIAN'S TOOLBOX

F OR MANY BUSINESS STUDENTS the subject of statistics is a necessary evil that has to be faced. This is probably because of the logically perverse way that statistics is unable to prove anything. All its power lies in its ability to *disprove* things. This means that, to use statistical techniques, you have to learn to think backwards. You must set up as true that which you hope to disprove, so that, if those techniques say the hypothesis can be rejected, you are left with the alternative – which is what you really wanted to prove in the first place. The problem is that you have not *proved* your pet theory, you have only shown that there is no evidence to *dis*prove it. This often feels like a rather empty victory.

Before you get too bogged down in the issues of null and alternative hypotheses or Type I and Type II errors, though, let's take a hard, cool look at why statistics can be useful.

Remember that if you want to use any of the tools that statistics makes available, then, provided you know the technique is possible, the mechanics of implementation and interpretation are easy to look up if you need to. You can consult a good textbook to clarify the limitations and assumptions of the method, or you can use the help systems of Excel or SPSS, two commonly available sets of analytical software, to find out how to do the sums. The key is knowing what is possible.

Statistics provides many useful tools apart from hypothesis-testing. It gives standard ways for plotting out data, standard ways of summarizing data and guides to what you should expect to see in particular situations.

Let's start with a few definitions.

STATISTICAL DEFINITIONS

Sampling

Life is too short to talk to everybody else in the world when you have a problem. If you are realistic you accept this, and only try to get in touch with a few people. But if you still want to know what the world believes, you've got to try to work it out from what the few people you talked to say (OK if you talk to reasonable people, but if you pick a bunch of weirdos you might have problems).

This is always difficult, because you will usually only be able to speak to a small sample of the whole population. There are, however, statistical methods that help you judge how far the people you talk to hold views which are common to the rest of the world.

Talking to a small group and then using what they tell you to work out what everybody else thinks is called sampling.

Population

A population is any group of people, or objects, that are similar in some way and form the subject of study of your survey. Populations can be finite or infinite. For example, the number of babies born in a given year is finite; the number of possible outcomes of tossing a coin for eternity, are potentially infinite.

Census

You conduct a census when you talk to every single person in your population – in formal speak, 'when a universe is examined in its entirety'. Censuses are expensive, relatively slow and comparatively rare.

Sample

Pick a few members of your population and examine them in detail. From what they tell you try and work out what the whole population thinks. Make sure that you choose your samples carefully, otherwise your guesses about the whole population will be nonsense.

Elementary sampling unit (ESU)

This is an individual element of the population that you are sampling: e.g. a certain sort of person (age, sex, etc.).

Sampling frame

The lists, indexes, maps or other records of a population that you use in order to pick your victims.

Statistic

Also known as an estimator, this is a descriptive number, calculated from a sample, that is used to estimate a population parameter. The parameter is the true but unknown value; the statistic is the mathematical guess you make, based on the response of your sample.

Parameter

This refers to the value of a variable calculated from the total population – i.e. the mean or average.

Sampling variability

Different samples drawn from the same population will have different statistics, because they were made up of different individuals, whereas for a given population, population parameters are the same every time, because the makeup of the population does not change.

Sampling distribution

A graph of the number of items in each sample, showing how many of each kind occur: e.g. 12 sample averages calculated and the 12 averages shown on a graph called a frequency distribution.

Stratified sample

A sample is specially designed so that you make sure that you pick the right sort of people for your sample. Usually you try to pick people who are a fair cross-section of the population you are interested in.

HOW TO TAKE A SAMPLE

PROBABILITY SAMPLING (RANDOM SAMPLING)

In this method every elementary sampling unit has an equal chance of being selected for the sample; once they are selected, you must interview or measure the individual or unit selected if the sample is to remain valid. Sometimes the impersonal-sounding 'elementary sampling units' are actually people, but they might be individual firms, or products or categories of representative data. In every case they are the smallest unit of respondent within your sample. There are a number of different ways of drawing a random sample.

There are two basic methods of sampling, probability sampling and non-probability sampling. With probability sampling, each unit has a known and equal chance of being included in the sample.

Simple random sampling

Done either by lottery or using random number generators. The essence of this technique is to avoid subjective bias arising from a personal choice of sampling unit.

Systematic or quasi-random sampling

The population to be surveyed is divided into groups with similar attributes. In each group or stratum the population is more nearly homogeneous than in the total population, and this contributes to the accuracy of the sampling process. Quotas are chosen for each group, and a representative quota is fixed. The members of the quota are chosen randomly.

Cluster sampling

A small number of groups or clusters are selected randomly, and every unit within the sample is interviewed. Cluster sampling is likely to increase the possibility of sample error being introduced, as clusters could exclude certain types of members of the population, but sometimes it is the only possible way to obtain data.

Multi-stage sampling

Multi-stage sampling involves selection at two or more successive stages. At each stage a sample (simple, stratified or otherwise) is taken, until the final sampling units are achieved. This does not require a sample frame covering the entire population. For example, the first stage of a national sample survey would divide the country by standard regions as classified by the Registrar General. Each region would involve selecting a sample of towns and rural districts, and then in the third stage a sample of individual respondents would be taken from the electoral registers of the second-stage area.

Master samples

Where you are likely to want to carry out repeated sampling of a static population, it is useful to construct a master random sample from which sub-samples, chosen at random, can be taken as required. The sampling units should be relatively permanently available to you, or else the value of the sample as a basis for comparison will decrease.

NON-PROBABILITY SAMPLING

With non-probability sampling, individual units in the population do not have an equal chance of appearing in the sample. Thus it is sometimes known as judgmental sampling, because the researcher's judgment is used to choose the sample rather than a statistical method. The researcher might go out to interview 25 young men between the ages of 20 and 30, choosing them personally because they looked male and the right age.

Quota sampling

This is the most common form of judgmental sample, where the biases arising from the method are controlled to some extent by stratification and the setting of quotas for each stratum. The population is divided into subgroups according to the requirements of the survey. Quotas are set by the researchers, and interviewers are given allocations of specific types of informants: e.g. interview 12 men and 12 women.

Characteristics of samples

How good an estimate of the population parameter is the Sample Statistic?

The theory of statistics allows us to estimate how well a sample will predict the value of a population parameter. We make use of Gauss's Central Limit Theorem (which I shall discuss later) to calculate confidence limits; the most commonly used are 95 per cent and 99 per cent confidence.

Accuracy of estimation v. sample size

It should be remembered that the relationship between the accuracy of the estimate obtained and the size of sample is a square-root relationship. This means that to improve the accuracy of your guess by a factor of two requires the sample size to be increased by four times.

THE SCOPE OF STATISTICAL ANALYSIS

Next we will take the lid off the toolbox and take a peek inside. Fortunately this toolbox is laid out in a logical order, so we will look at each tool in turn and see what it can do (see Figure 5.1).

UNDERSTANDING YOUR PROJECT DATA SET

Data types

Your project data will consist of three possible types.

1. **Continuous Numerical Data**. Numbers which can take any value between plus and minus infinity, having as many possible values between 0 and 1 as there are between 0 and infinity.
2. **Integer Numerical Data**. Numbers which can only take whole values: i.e. 1, 2, 3, etc. No fractions are possible within a set of integer data.
3. **Qualitative Data**. These are data which do not have a numerical value: for example, gender (male/female) or attitude to a

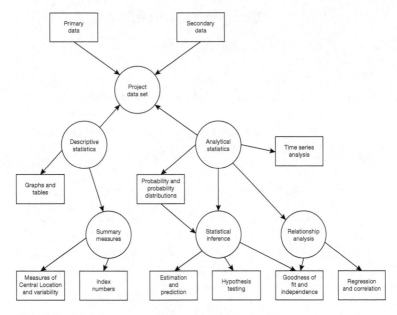

Figure 5.1
A Range of Statistical Tools: The Contents of the Toolbox

proposition (yes/no). These data are generally split into categories by the researcher, and hence are known as categorical data. Some categorical data can be arranged into logical orders as shown below:

- **Using a nominal scale** This is the least sophisticated type of scale. It involves simple classification by the attributes you are interested in, which are then turned into numbers so your computer can sort them. (You need to do this, as computers don't understand things like sex but do understand 1 standing for female and 2 for male.) You can use this type of coding for any non-numeric properties and can make up numbers for almost any population characteristic you can imagine and then share it with your computer.
- **Using an ordinal scale** This is a ranking scale which lists the objects you are studying according to certain character-

istics that you choose (e.g. colour of hair). As there is no way of measuring the distance between objects, the statistical techniques you can use are limited to positional measures, which help represent the *order* data appear in. Typical examples are median, quartile, percentile, etc.

- **Using an interval scale** Interval scales can also be called cardinal scales. This is because you make them up from a line of points you think are important. If you choose your points so they are equal distances apart you will know something about distance between points as well as the order they appear in. If you use interval scales to collect your data, you can work out statistical measures, such as the arithmetic mean, standard deviation, correlation coefficient and other tests of significance.

HOW TO CAPTURE CATEGORICAL DATA

Likert scaling

This uses either three or five reactions – from the range *strongly agree, agree, uncertain, disagree, strongly disagree* – to a particular statement. It does not produce an interval scale but gives a ranking order for the responses you have collected.

Semantic differential scale

Respondents are asked to rate a number of objects or concepts along a continuum – e.g.

Fair . . . . . . Unfair.

Weights are assigned to continuum positions, and, as the respondent fixes the neutral point, it can produce an interval scale if you choose your weighting factors in such a way that the inferred neutral point is central to the scale.

DESCRIPTIVE STATISTICS

TABLES

Frequency table

Tabulation (sorting the data into tables) is the first step in categorizing your set of research data. The simplest form of table is a frequency table. This lists your data in the groups you have set up, so that you can see patterns. For example, it might show the number of male respondents, the number of female respondents and the total number of respondents. Drawing up an initial set of frequency tables helps you see what data you have collected and often shows up strange entries (i.e. misspellings or silly numbers), which end up in a group of their own which you didn't expect to be there!

Relative frequency table

A relative frequency table shows the proportions of each group, so that the total number of fractions totals the whole set.

Cross-tabulation table

This tabulates two or more groups of data against each other. For example, when you have collected data about eye colour and gender, a cross-tabulation table (known as a cross-tab) will show you how many males of each eye colour you have, how females of each eye colour and the total number of each gender and each eye colour.

GRAPHS AND CHARTS

Line graph

A line graph is a way of showing a series of numerical data points which vary with respect to some other variable, often time. It helps you visualize changes in the data and spot trends and movements which are not always obvious when looking at tables of data.

Line chart

A line chart takes categorical data as its input and displays it equally spaced along the X-axis. It differs from a line graph in that (as in a bar chart) the length of line represents a count of the occurrences of each category that has been observed, not a measured value (e.g. the number of red-haired people, rather than a measured average height). This produces useful comparison charts for non-numeric data.

Bar chart

A bar chart displays numerical values of different data variables showing their relationship by means of the height or length of either lines or rectangles of equal width. Bar charts can be drawn with their lines or rectangles plotted vertically or horizontally.

Histogram

This is a summary graph which shows a count of any data points falling in ranges you choose. It shows a rough approximation of the frequency distribution of the data you are plotting. The ranges you choose are called 'classes', and you can think of them as dump bins or containers that accumulate data and 'fill up' at a rate which is a measure of the number of times the chosen data class occurs.

Frequency polygon

A frequency polygon is a graph of the frequency table for the data. Your classes (if the data are categorical) are shown on the X-axis and the number of hits in each class is represented by the height of a point located above the middle of that class. The points are linked by straight lines so that, together with the X-axis, they sketch out a polygon – hence the name.

Cumulative frequency charts

A cumulative frequency chart displays cumulative totals for a set of values, adding each point to the total of the previous points on the chart. It is a way of presenting information visually, and allows you to visualize the pattern of the data. For example, you can see the median (or middle) of the data. You can also observe the upper and lower quartile points as well as the interquartile range from the display.

Pie charts

Famously invented by Florence Nightingale as a way of displaying the problems of military nursing during the Crimean War, the pie chart is circular (pie-shaped), and the pie is split into segments which represent percentages or the relative contributions of different categories of data.

Pictograms

This is a way of showing quantities by drawing a cartoon picture of the subject. This technique is limited to the presentation of simple relationships, but it can be a powerful visual aid to a business presentation – perhaps when pitching for the new generation of nuclear power stations (e.g. one nuclear power station surrounded by images of the million windmills it can replace, perhaps showing the area of land required to be covered by windmills in order to match the continuous power output).

Logarithmic graphs

Logarithmic graphs are useful when you need to display data which has an accelerating rate of change. By plotting it using a log scale, the rate of change of the acceleration is displayed: constant acceleration showing as a straight line, and increasing or decreasing acceleration as a curved logarithmic graph.

Scatter graphs

A scatter graph displays two sets of data, one on the Y-axis the other on the X, and shows if there is any correlation between them. It is a particularly useful graph for looking at business data where you suspect there might be a relationship, but are not sure. If the points form a line, then it is possible there is a relationship; if they are randomly scattered, it is clear that there is no relationship.

SUMMARY MEASURES

Summary measures are numerical ways to summarize large sets of data. They fall into two types: measures of location – which give an idea of where the 'centre of gravity' of the data is situated within the data set – and measures of spread, dispersion or variability – which give an idea of how widely scattered the data is about its 'centre of gravity'.

MEASURES OF LOCATION

There are four commonly used measures of location:

Arithmetic mean

The arithmetic mean is the average of a set of n numbers. You calculate it by adding the numbers together and dividing by n. The statistic only works with numerical data.

Mode

The mode is the value that occurs most frequently in a data set. It can be used for both numerical and categorical data.

Median

The median is the value within an ordered data set that divides it in half. That is to say, it is the middle value of a sequence of data arranged in order of magnitude. You can use it with numerical data or ranked categorical data.

Geometric mean

The geometric mean is the logarithmic average value of a data set. Unlike an arithmetic mean, it tends to dampen the effect of extreme high or low values, which might bias the result if an arithmetic mean is calculated. This is helpful for financial investment return calculations. The geometric mean is calculated on the decimal multiplier equivalent values, not percentage values (e.g. a 6 per cent increase becomes 1.06; a 3 per cent decline is transformed to 0.97).

To calculate the geometric mean multiply n data values together and take the nth root of the result (e.g. the geometric mean of 2 and 3 is the square root of 6: i.e. 2.449).

MEASURES OF SPREAD

There are a number of statistical values which offer useful ways to summarize how widely the data set is spread around its 'centre of gravity'.

RANGE

The statistical range is the difference between the lowest and highest values in a numerical data set. You calculate it by first sorting the data set into order and then subtracting the smallest value from the largest.

Quartiles

These are the three values in a numerical data set that divide it into four equal parts. Moving from the lowest value to the highest, the **lower quartile** sits at the top of the lowest 25 per cent of the data; **the median** is halfway through the data, and the **upper quartile** lies at the bottom of the top 25 per cent of the data.

Interquartile range

The interquartile range is the difference between the upper quartile and the lower quartile, so it is a measure of the spread of the middle 50 per cent of the data. It has the advantage that it is not affected by extreme values.

Semi-interquartile range

The semi-interquartile range is half the difference between the upper quartile and the lower quartile. It is half the distance needed to cover half the data values. In a symmetric distribution, an interval stretching from one semi-interquartile range below the median to one semi-interquartile above it will contain half the scores. It is not greatly affected by extreme scores, so it is a good measure of spread for skewed distributions. However, it is more sensitive to sampling fluctuation in normal distributions than standard deviation, and so is not often used for data that are normally distributed.

Deciles

These are like quartiles, but they divide a sequential numerical data set into ten equal parts.

Interdecile range

This term is the difference in data values between the first and ninth deciles. Like the interquartile range, it provides an indication of the spread of the data set, but it covers the middle 80 per cent. It is not widely used.

Interpercentile range

The interpercentile range is the difference in value between any to two chosen percentiles (a percentile being the point below or above which a chosen proportion of an observation is located). The interdecile range is an example of an interpercentile range between the upper and lower 10 percentile points in a sequential numerical data set. For an interpercentile range you are free to choose your own intervals.

It is a stable measure of spread (unless one of the select points is the minimum or maximum of the data set), and its value can be worked out with relatively few iterations. It has the advantage of providing a consistent interpretation between distributions. Be aware, however, that, if you apply an interpercentile range calculation to a discrete distribution (particularly one where there are only a few important values), it can give odd and inaccurate results.

MEAN DEVIATION

The mean deviation is the average of the modulus of the differences (this means the differences expressed without a plus or minus sign) between each value in a data set of values, and the average of all values of that data set. It is sometimes a useful measure when the number of values in the data set is small. If you've got plenty of data points, then standard deviation is a better measure.

STANDARD DEVIATION

The standard deviation is the square root of the arithmetic average of the sum of the squares of the deviations from the mean in a data set.

VARIANCE

The variance is the square of the standard deviation. It is thus the arithmetic average of the sum of the squares of the deviations from the mean in a data set.

COEFFICIENT OF VARIATION

This is defined at the standard deviation of a data set divided by its mean. For business problems, it serves as a rough measure of relative risk. It is also known as Pearson's coefficient of variation, after its inventor, Karl Pearson.

INDEX NUMBERS

An index number is used to indicate changes in values over a data set (usually over time) – such as prices, wages, employment levels, etc. – relative to a chosen start point that is usually standardized at 100. They can also be used to plot changes in groups of related data sets. Perhaps the best known example is the Retail Prices Index, which is defined by the UK government as follows:

> The Retail Prices Index (RPI) is the most familiar general purpose domestic measure of inflation in the United Kingdom. It is available continuously from June 1947. The Government uses it for uprating of pensions, benefits and index-linked gilts. It is commonly used in private contracts for uprating of mainten-ance payments and housing rents. It is also used for wage bargaining.

ANALYTIC STATISTICS

WHAT IS PROBABILITY?

Probability is a branch of mathematics that deals with calculating the likelihood of a given event's occurrence, which is expressed as a number between 1 and 0. An event with a probability of 1 is a certainty: for example, the probability of a coin toss resulting in either 'heads' or 'tails' is 1, because there are no other options, assuming the coin lands flat. An event with a probability of a half has equal odds of occurring or not occurring: for example, the probability of a coin toss resulting in 'heads' is half, because the toss is equally likely to result in 'tails'. An event with a probability of 0 is impossible: for example, the probability that the coin will land (flat) without either side facing up is 0, because either 'heads' or 'tails' must be facing up.

Probability theory attempts to undertake precise calculations about uncertain and random events.

In its simplest form, probability can be calculated as the number of occurrences of the target event divided by the number of all possible outcomes.

THE ALGEBRA OF PROBABILITIES

Addition rule of probabilities

The addition rule determines the probability that event A or event B occurs, or if both occur.

The result is, using set notation:

$$P(A \cup B) = P(A) + P(B) - P(A \cap B)$$

where:

   $P(A)$ = probability that event A occurs
   $P(B)$ = probability that event B occurs
   $P(A \cup B)$ = probability that event A or event B occurs
   $P(A \cap B)$ = probability that event A *and* event B both occur

For mutually exclusive events (events which cannot occur together):

$$P(A \cap B) = 0$$

The addition rule is then:

$$P(A \cup B) = P(A) + P(B)$$

For independent events (events which have no influence on each other):

$$P(A \cap B) = P(A).P(B)$$

The addition rule is then:

$$P(A \cup B) = P(A) + P(B) - P(A).P(B)$$

Conditional probability

When I have lots of information about an event, I am able to revise my guess about the probability of further events happening. Suppose

I go to lunch at the same place and time every Friday, and I'm served lunch within 15 minutes with probability 0.9. However, if the restaurant is busy, the probability of my getting lunch within 15 minutes may reduce to 0.7. This is the conditional probability of my being served lunch within 15 minutes, given that the restaurant is busy.

The standard way of writing 'event A occurs, given that event B has occurred' is 'A|B' (said as 'the probability of A given B'). The symbol | is a vertical line which does not imply division.

P(A|B) is simply a way to write the probability that event A will occur, given that event B has already happened.

The rule for calculating a conditional probability from unconditional probabilities is:

$$P(A|B) = \frac{P(A \cap B)}{P(B)}$$

where:

P(A|B) = the (conditional) probability that event A will occur, given that event B has occurred already;

P(A∩B) = the (unconditional) probability that event A *and* event B both occur;

P(B) = the (unconditional) probability that event B occurs.

Multiplication rule of probability

The multiplication rule is used to calculate the probability of two events, A and B, both occurring. It follows from the definition of conditional probability. The result is often written as follows, using set notation:

P(A∩B) = P(A|B).P(B) or P(A∩B) = P(B|A).P(A)

where:

P(A) = probability that event A occurs;

P(B) = probability that event B occurs;

P(A∩B) = probability that event A *and* event B occur;

P(A | B) = the conditional probability that event A occurs, given that event B has occurred already;

P(B | A) = the conditional probability that event B occurs, given that event A has occurred already.

For independent events this becomes:

$$P(A \cap B) = P(A).P(B)$$

That is, the probability of the joint events A and B is equal to the individual probabilities for the two events multiplied together.

Bayes' rule for conditional probabilities

Bayes' rule says that the probability P(E|A) of some event E, given that another event A has been observed, is:

$$P(E)P(A|E)/P(A)$$

where:

P(E) is the prior probability of E, determined either objectively or subjectively; and

P(A), the probability of A, is given by the sum over all possible events Ej of the quantity $P(E_j)P(A|E_j)$.

Bayesian probability problems are often solved using branching tree diagrams, which are also useful for clarifying the logic of interlinked events.

To use this algebra of probabilities you need to work out values for the various probabilities. There are three basic ways of doing this.

SUBJECTIVE PROBABILITY

This is simply a guess, based on your personal judgment, of how likely a particular event is to occur. It is not based on any precise calculation but may be a reasonable assessment if done by a knowledgeable person with experience in the field.

A subjective probability is expressed on a scale from 0 to 1; a rare event has a subjective probability close to 0, a common event has a subjective probability close to 1. Your subjective probability of an event describes your degree of belief in the event occurring.

Probability by experiment

We can guess about the future by counting how often things have happened in the past. So I can test a coin by tossing it ten times and recording the results:

T H T H H T T T H H

Out of ten trials I get five heads and five tails. From this experiment I can safely say the likelihood of tossing a head is five chances in ten or $\frac{5}{10}$, which is 0.5. Or can I?

If I had only tossed the coin eight times, I would have had five tails and three heads for eight trials. So then I would have been forced to think that the likelihood of tossing a head is three chances in eight or $\frac{3}{8}$, which is 0.375. (We may have to think about that result later.)

The name for this way of working out the likelihood is called calculating the posterior probability. You can use the method whenever you have a lot of data about what really happened. For example, insurance companies use data on death rates to calculate the premiums that you will be charged for life insurance. By looking at the number of people within an age range and the number of deaths there were, a probability can be counted.

I could use data from a questionnaire to work out the probability of having blue eyes. Say I get 162 usable questionnaires for eye colour, and, out of those, 64 report they had blue eyes. If I then choose a person at random, there are 64 chances out of 162 that they will have blue eyes. That is a posterior probability of $\frac{64}{162}$, which works out at 0.395, or about two chances in every five people of finding blue eyes.

Similarly, I can work out the probability of having blonde hair. Say I have 39 people with blonde hair out of the same 162 question-naires. That gives a probability of $\frac{39}{162}$, which works out as 0.24, or about one chance in four of finding somebody with blonde hair at random.

If I now want to use this information to try to guess how many individuals in the country have blue eyes, I can do it in three steps:

1. I can assume my sample is typical of all the population of the country.
2. Next I work out the ratio of blue-eyed individuals in the sample (0.4).
3. I multiply the number of people in the country by this fraction (0.4), and this is my prediction of the number of blue-eyed individuals.

This guess will work quite well, provided I did not sample just a set of blue-eyed freaks, when the rest of the world really all has green eyes. It is good practice to guard against mistakes of this kind by always making sure you write down the assumptions you make in this type of forecast.

Probability by logic

You may have noticed that when I took only my first eight trials for tossing the coin I worked out the probability of tossing a head was 0.375. This may be true if the coin is biased but if it is not you would be right to be suspicious of this result. The reason lies in the logic of the situation. The coin has two sides, and only one can show at any time. It must therefore end up either as a head or a tail. If the coin is unbiased, there is just as much chance of a head outcome as there is of a tail one. Logic tells us that we can have only one outcome from two possible states. There can only be one chance in two of any outcome happening. This is a calculated probability of one chance in two of tossing a head. That is a probability of ½, or 0.5, of tossing a head.

Here I am not using any experimental data; I am reasoning how many outcomes there can possibly be, and then working out the chances of any single outcome happening. The jargon for this is an 'a priori probability'.

Think about a die. There are six faces that can come up when the die is rolled. The chance of throwing a One is 1 chance in 6. That is a probability of ⅙, which works out to be 0.167.

Table 5.1
All the Ways Two Dice Can Fall

Die One	Die Two	Total	Die One	Die Two	Total
1	1	2	4	1	5
1	2	3	4	2	6
1	3	4	4	3	7
1	4	5	4	4	8
1	5	6	4	5	9
1	6	7	4	6	10
2	1	3	5	1	6
2	2	4	5	2	7
2	3	5	5	3	8
2	4	6	5	4	7
2	5	7	5	5	10
2	6	8	5	6	11
3	1	4	6	1	7
3	2	5	6	2	8
3	3	6	6	3	9
3	4	7	6	4	10
3	5	8	6	5	11
3	6	9	6	6	12

In any situation where I can work out all the outcomes, we can use this form of reasoning. If we throw two dice, there are 36 ways they can fall.

If I draw these possible scores from the two dice as a frequency chart, I get Figure 5.2.

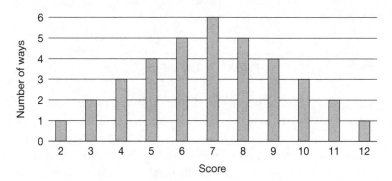

Figure 5.2
Frequency Histogram for the Fall of Two Dice

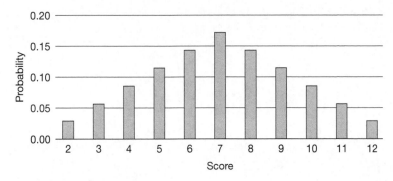

Figure 5.3
Probability Chart for the Fall of Two Dice

From this I can work out the probability of throwing any score using the two dice (see Figure 5.3). For example, the probability of throwing Seven is 6 chances in 36, which works out as ⁶⁄₃₆, or 0.167, which is the same odds as throwing any number on a single die. But the chances of throwing a Double Six and scoring 12 is much less. It is only 1 chance in 36, which works out as ¹⁄₃₆, or 0.0278.

Notice the bell shape of the frequency diagram. If I divided each number of ways of throwing a particular number by the total number of outcomes I would get a picture of the probability of throwing any particular score.

But these are integer outcomes, and integer outcomes cannot be split up (i.e. 2.5 children is not a real possibility). Most real business data tend to be continuous data, which leads me into the use of continuous probability distributions.

PROBABILITY DISTRIBUTIONS

Probability distributions are mathematical models which accurately describe the situation associated with particular events that might interest us. They have defined mathematical properties and are widely used for drawing inferences in business; quality control, in particular, makes great use of probability distributions. In practice, many business situations can be shown to have the same under-lying probability structure, and so can be represented by the same probability distribution. There are three probability distributions which have widespread applications to a range of business problems.

BINOMIAL DISTRIBUTION

The binomial distribution is a probability distribution for integer data. It is used when there are only two mutually exclusive outcomes of a trial – usually called Success and Failure. The binomial distribution is used to obtain the probability of observing R successes in N trials, with the probability of success in a single trial denoted by P.

The distribution is calculated using the following formula:

$$P(X = R) = {}_NC_R \, P^R(1 - P)^{N-R}$$

where:

N = Number of events;
R = Number of successful events;
P = Probability of success in a single trial.

$NCR = (N! \, / \, (N - R)!) \, / \, R!$

$1 - P$ = Probability of failure.

Often you can summarize a group of independent observations by the number of observations in the group that represent one of two outcomes. For example, the proportion of individuals in a random sample who choose one of two possible products fits this description. In this case, the statistic $\hat{P}$ is the count X of subjects who chose product 1, divided by the total number of individuals in the group N. This provides an estimate of the parameter P, the proportion of individuals who will choose product 1 in the entire population.

The binomial distribution describes the behaviour of a count variable X if the following conditions apply:

- The number of observations N is fixed;
- Each observation is independent;
- Each observation represents one of two outcomes ('success' or 'failure');
- The probability of 'success' P is the same for each outcome.

If these conditions are met, then X has a binomial distribution with parameters N and P, and is written as $B(N, P)$ and has a Mean = $N*P$ and a Variance = $N*P*(1 - P)$.

POISSON DISTRIBUTION

The Poisson distribution describes the behaviour of integer random data sets in terms of probabilities of the number of events likely to happen in a chosen unit of time. Unlike the binomial distribution, it is not symmetrical, as it is skewed to the left of the median. You can use it when the probability of an event is small and the number of opportunities for that event is large (e.g. the probability distribution of misprints in a book). The Poisson distribution is an extension of the binomial distribution and can be used as an approximation to it. Its standard deviation equals the square root of the mean.

The Poisson distribution has two main applications in business problems:

1. It can be used as an alternative to the binomial distribution in the case of very large samples. The types of event could be the number of cases of a rare disease, the number of accidents on a busy junction, the number of stoppages on a production line, or the number of a particular socio-economic group attending a football match. It can also be used to test if the environmental and other factors influencing an event are constant between observation periods.

   The main difference between the Poisson distribution and the binomial distribution is that in the binomial all eligible phenomena are studied, whereas in the Poisson distribution only the cases with a particular outcome are studied. For example: in the binomial all cars are studied to see whether they have had an accident or not, whereas using the Poisson distribution only the cars which have an accident are studied.

2. The Poisson distribution can also be used to study how 'accidents' or 'malfunctions' – or the chance of winning the national lottery never, once or more than once – are distributed on the level of a population. This makes it useful for statistical studies of quality

and insurance risk. If having an 'accident' has no influence on the chance of having another accident, the subject is 'put back into the population' immediately after the 'event'. People may have one, two, three, or more accidents during a certain period of time. (For accident you could substitute mistakes causing a quality failure in a product line, for example.) The Poisson distribution tells you how these chances are distributed.

NORMAL DISTRIBUTION

The normal distribution helps you predict behaviour in continuous data sets. It is a bell-shaped symmetrical frequency distribution which is found in many economic, natural, social and other real-world phenomena (such as IQ scores, height variation within a population, weights of crop yields, variation in quality of manufactured goods, etc.). It occurs in circumstances where two or more variables have a direct relationship and high predictability (low variation). Extremely large and extremely small values are rare in the normal distribution and only occur near the tail ends. The most frequently occurring values cluster round the mean (which, as the distribution is symmetrical, is the same as the median and mode) and fall off smoothly in either side of it. In the normal distribution, 68 per cent of all values lie within one standard deviation, 95.45 per cent within two standard deviations, and 99.8 per cent within three standard deviations (called six sigma in quality control). In other words, only one out of a thousand values will fall outside the Six-Sigma range.[3]

A German lad called Carl Friedrich Gauss, who was born in Brunswick in 1777 and became Professor of Mathematics at Göttingen in 1795 at the age of 18, discovered this distribution. He found that a lot of natural events have probabilities which can be predicted by a shape he called the Normal Distribution.

He worked out what he called a Law of Errors of Direct Measurement using a principle known a maximum likelihood. It eventually became known as the Central Limit Theorem (see Figure 5.4). This law

3   Six-Sigma is the name used by Motorola for its total quality management system.

Figure 5.4
The Normal Probability
Integral

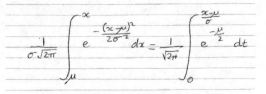

$$\frac{1}{\sigma\sqrt{2\pi}} \int_{\mu}^{x} e^{-\frac{(x-\mu)^2}{2\sigma^2}} dx = \frac{1}{\sqrt{2\pi}} \int_{0}^{\frac{x-\mu}{\sigma}} e^{-\frac{\mu}{2}} dt$$

became very important for statistics, because it makes possible the forecasting of errors in sampling continuous variables (like height) from a population. It just so happened that the distribution he discovered also explains a lot of naturally occurring populations. We use the distribution everywhere in quality measurements and in forecasting future events.

That's the good news. The bad news is that the normal distribution involves fairly heavy sums to work it out.

Fortunately, though, Gauss worked out all the important values and published them in sets of tables. We still use this table of values, and can use either Excel or SPSS to look them up for us. Every Normal Distribution we will ever want can be found once we work out the mean and the standard deviation of our sample.

Gauss's table is for a normal distribution with a mean of 0 and a standard deviation of 1. This is written in Statistics jargon as $N(0,1)$. If we want to use it for other distributions we have to carry out a bit of arithmetic fiddling. This is called standardization.

Here's a picture of Gauss's normal distribution (Figure 5.5).

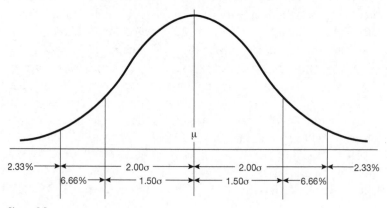

Figure 5.5
The Gaussian Normal Distribution

His Central Limit Theorem says that under general conditions the average values of data sets observed over time tend to be distributed as a normal distribution. That is to say, if you take samples from a population, the means of those samples (provided they are of 30 or more events) follow a normal distribution. This property implies that, no matter how a variable changes, the sum of its values will show a normal distribution if enough sets of sample measurements are taken. It also leads to the theory of confidence limits, which allows predictions of the likely range of errors in your measurements.

TIME SERIES ANALYSIS

Time series analysis is a family of techniques that all make the same underlying assumption: that the only independent variable that needs to be considered is time. The use of time as a proxy variable to simplify the complexity that exists in reality results in methods that are arithmetically straightforward and simple to use. Nonetheless, even though some of the time series techniques are extremely simple, they are capable of yielding highly accurate results, provided they are applied in the correct circumstances.

TIME AS A PROXY

A proxy variable is a variable that is used instead of the real independent variable in order to simplify the analysis. This may be because the real independent variable has not been identified, or it may be because a more accurate representation of the situation would be too difficult to apply mathematical analysis to.

There are dangers in using time as the independent variable – in that you might come to think of results occurring simply *because* time has passed. Remember that sales are caused by the actions of customers deciding to make a purchase, and this decision is dependent on many things apart from the passage of time. Wherever possible, you should clearly state the reasons why you are using time as a proxy variable and, if possible, you should outline the actual causes of the levels of demand that you are predicting. Although a forecast predicts a level of demand, that forecast makes certain assumptions that a plan of action might well seek to change. In asking the question, 'what are the real causes of demand fluctuation', you should also list the assumptions you have made. Likewise, in planning a course of action in the light of the forecast demand, you will usually seek both to question and perhaps to change the assumptions used. Without accurate knowledge of your assumptions, any users of your solutions have less scope for corrective action, because you have not clearly defined the ground rules for change. A forecast that assumes that sales come about simply because time has elapsed gives any manager who must use the forecast little guidance as to possible areas of influence that might change business prospects, and presents the forecast as an inescapable fate.

Identifying the historical data pattern

Before choosing which technique to use, it is useful to identify the nature of any data patterns that have appeared in past data. I have already discussed the fundamental patterns that occur in most data series, and I suggest you make sure you are familiar with the three main patterns (stationary, trend and cyclical) before attempting to apply time series analysis.

Once the basic patterns are familiar, the simplest way of deciding which pattern has been apparent in the past is to plot the data on a suitable graph and study the picture produced, looking for similarities with the three basic patterns. The choice of scale of both the dependent and independent variables is critical in this exercise. When considering the dependent variable, too large a scale will enhance minor random variations, while too cramped a scale will reduce all data to a stationary series. Likewise, when considering the independent variable (which in this case is always time), too extended a scale will mask the occurrence of long-term cyclical variations that could be important for the accuracy of the forecast. When attempting pattern recognition in a new data set, it is advisable to experiment with a range of scales, in order to ensure that you do not overlook the obvious.

Be aware that a certain amount of random variation is to be expected in any real data, and wherever possible try to picture the pattern underlying any random excursions that may be superimposed on the graph. One simple way to improve your pattern-recognition skills is to sketch a smooth curve through the data points in order to study the shape of the data with its randomness reduced. But take care not force a preconceived data pattern on to information that does not support it.

HOW TO ANALYSE STATIONARY DATA

MOVING AVERAGES

A problem frequently encountered is preparing short-term forecasts for a large number of different items. The cost of developing individually tailored methods of forecasting for each of the individual products is prohibitive in time and money, so a technique is needed that can be employed easily for several items and will provide accurate short-term forecasts.

If you can make a basic assumption that the historical sales data may be represented by a stationary time series, you can use an estimate of the mean value as a predictor. The simplest technique of this type is the moving average.

A horizontal data pattern varies about an average (or mean) value in some sort of random manner. The best forecast of the next period's sales is then the mean value. To obtain an estimate of the mean value you just 'smooth' out the humps in the historical data. If there is a lot of randomness (or variation) in the past data, simply taking the most recent observation as the new forecast will result in an inaccurate forecast. To get a better estimate, a number of past sales figures must be averaged out. If, for example, the average of the three most recent sales figures is taken, this will give you an estimate of the mean which you can use as your forecast for the coming period. As time goes on, the latest sales figures are added and the earliest subtracted. This method is known as a moving-average forecast, because the average moves along the lines of data points.

EXPONENTIAL SMOOTHING

The moving-average technique does not respond quickly to sudden changes in sales. If a 'turning point' occurs (e.g. the sales trend changes from, say, upward to downward) it can take one or two forecasting periods before this change is reflected in the forecast. The moving average is slow to react to changes, because it gives equal weight to all the values that go to make up the forecast. If, for example, the sales have been 900 items for two consecutive months, and then the next month's sales drop to 300, a moving-average forecast (window = 3) for the following month will be:

$$Forecast = 900 + 900 + 300 = 700$$

This formula can be rewritten to show clearly the weighting:

$$Forecast = 1/3*(900) + 1/3*(900) + 1/3*(300) = 300 + 300 + 100$$
$$= 700$$

This shows that each of the previous three months' sales data contribute one-third of the forecast, and each of the previous data items has equal weight in the final value of the forecast. The more points are included in a forecast, the less notice is taken of the newest and most up-to-date information. Since the most recent observations contain the most information about what will happen in the future, I can argue that they should be given relatively more weight than the older information. To improve the accuracy I can use a weighting scheme that will apply most weight to the most recent observed values and decreasing weights to the older ones. A technique that is simple to use and which satisfies this requirement is called exponential smoothing.

This operates similarly to moving averages by 'smoothing' historical observations to eliminate randomness. The equation for an exponentially smoothed forecast is:

$$forecast = previous\ forecast + \alpha\ (actual\ sales - previous\ forecast)$$

The new forecast is simply the old forecast plus α times the error in the old forecast (where α is a number in the range 0–1). If α has a value close to 1, then the new forecast will include a substantial adjustment for any error that occurred in the preceding forecast. Conversely, when α is close to 0, the new forecast will not show a large adjustment for the error of the old one. The effect, therefore, of a large or small α is similar to the effect of including a small or a large number of observations in the moving-average forecast.

You must choose the value of α to suit your data set and your question. There is no simple rule for selecting it; the value is chosen by a mixture of experience, and trial and error.

Two items of past data are required in order to produce forecasts:

- the previous forecast;
- the latest actual sales figure.

HOW TO CALCULATE TRENDS

The techniques that have been discussed so far have assumed that the underlying data set is horizontal. This is not always the case. Most business data exhibit a trend. The technique of trend analysis fits a straight line through the data points and uses this straight line to project a forecast for the coming period. The problem is how to fit the trend line to the past data that are available. Here are two simple methods:

- fitting by eye using graphical methods;
- fitting by the method of least squares (linear regression).

The method I describe uses only graph paper, a ruler and a few sums (it can be done on the back of an envelope during a meeting, if necessary, to check wild claims).

The mathematical equation which describes a straight line is written as:

$$y = mx + c$$

where m and c are the parameters of the line, y is the dependent variable, and x is time, the independent variable. These two parameters describe fully a line that can be drawn by eye through the data.

The parameter c describes the intercept with the Y-axis and is found by measuring the point where the line cuts the Y-axis (see Figure 5.6).

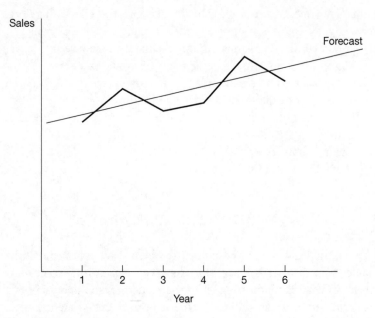

Figure 5.6
A Set of Sales Data

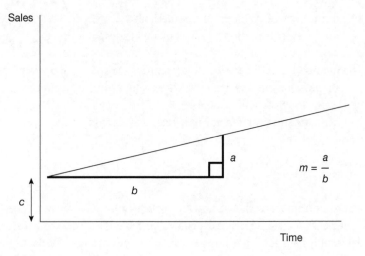

$$m = \frac{a}{b}$$

Figure 5.7
Calculating a Trend Line

The parameter m, which is a measure of the slope or steepness of the line, is found by measuring the simple triangle shown in Figure 5.7.

In general, the more past data points are available, the more accurate the forecast is likely to be, providing the underlying trend remains constant. As a rule of thumb, five data points are the minimum needed in order to get a good estimate of a trend line (see Figure 5.7). (NB For saturating or exponential trends this technique can be used on log data v. time.)

Both Excel and SPSS incorporate curve-fitting programs which apply this method using regression analysis (least squares best fit).

SEASONALITY

If your data set contains regular seasonal variations, and you need to predict, then you need a practical way to cope with the cyclical nature of the data. One way is to make use of the knowledge that the seasonal (yearly), and to some extent cyclical (longer than a year), fluctuations tend to be regular. If the data can be separated out into sets which exhibit either a horizontal or a trend pattern, then simple techniques can be used. This technique is called data partition or decomposition, and it enables the seasonality, or cyclical, component to be separated from either the horizontal or trend component, thus greatly simplifying the calculations.

By removing the seasonality factor in this way it is possible to produce useful forecasts (predictions). If this simple partitioning trick fails to work you might need to fall back onto Fourier analysis, which fits a combination of sine and cosine waves to the pattern. Look in the curve-fitting sections of SPSS for these techniques.

STATISTICAL INFERENCE

In order to answer a number of different business problems you might need to draw an inference about a population based on your measurement of a sample of that population. To do this successfully you need to address two main issues. The first is how to predict unknown values of a population parameter (e.g. How big is the market for Brand X?).

The second is to test an hypothesis about the values of the population parameter you have previously estimated (e.g. Does Brand X appeal more strongly to Asian women or middle-aged black men?). The two most commonly encountered population parameters which you need to deal with are the mean and the variance.

ESTIMATING AND PREDICTING

HOW RELIABLE ARE ESTIMATES BASED ON LIMITED-SIZE SAMPLES?

We would all like certainty in our business dealings, and yet we can only have probabilities.

If I say there is a probability of 75 per cent that we will make a profit, it sounds like a fine answer to give, but what does it actually mean? It means that, if I were a gambling man, I would give you odds of three to one on that I might be right. But it also means I have doubts; I worry that about one time in four I am going to be wildly wrong.

If your business question involves prediction you have to manage the uncertainty this implies. We tend to pride ourselves on the logical and scientific way in which we tackle the problems of running a business. We *analyse* markets, we *manage* investments, we *control* quality. All these standard business terms suggest that we can be completely on top of what is going on, but we are fooling ourselves if we believe that.

As Mark Twain said, 'There are only two certainties in this life, Death and Taxes'. All other business information is only certain after it has happened – far too late for us to use it to *manage* the future. How can we cope with such uncertainty about our research questions?

Uncertainty even spreads into our attempts to find out what is happening now. Complete knowledge involves collecting and processing vast amounts of data. To be certain about any question we must ask everybody in a complete population to answer us. A total census is extremely expensive in both time and money, so often we have to compromise, and we only have a sample to work with. From that sample we must try and guess how the complete population will respond.

When you obtain data from a sample, there will be an element of sampling error, or uncertainty, about the estimates of population parameters you calculate. These sampling errors occur because your actual sample is only one of a large number of possible samples, each of which would have given rise to a different estimate. All your population estimates are subject to sampling error, or uncertainty, since they have to be based on a sample of individuals rather than a census of the whole population.

It is possible to say how precise an estimate is by using the Central Limit Theorem to calculate a confidence interval around your guess to show a range of values within which lies the true population value (the value you would measure if you tested the whole population). Confidence intervals are normally calculated as 95 per cent or 99 per cent confidence intervals. For 95 per cent confidence, in 19 samples out of 20 we would expect the true value to lie within the confidence range we have calculated. For 99 per cent intervals this becomes 99 out of 100.

What you need to know is how to make the best possible guess using the information you have.

THE LIMITS OF UNCERTAINTY

If you are to make predictions about business decisions you have to think about a whole range of outcomes. There are three, though, which matter to you most. These are the Worst Case, the Best Case and the Most Likely Case.

When you are planning or predicting you have to make sure you try to predict the worst outcome you can imagine. I suggest you remember the extremely helpful and reliable 'Sod's Law': usually stated in the form 'A jam butty always hits the floor jam-side down'. There are variations on this, such as what is often known as Murphy's Law: 'Whatever can go wrong will go wrong'.

Both laws contain a Truth you need to remember. Business predictions often fail because the researcher has assumed that fortune will smile on the business. When it does not, you will wish you had provided a contingency for when things go wrong.

So how are we going to turn these vague worries about possible disasters into usable estimates? The work of Gauss will help us; he spotted a very odd thing about samples and averages. If you take a series of samples then the probability distribution of the samples is a normal distribution. If our sample guess happened to be the lowest possible, then the normal distribution surrounding it would still just include the true mean. The same would apply if our guess happened to be the highest possible value. So, even at extreme values, we will still be right in guessing the range which includes the mean in 95 cases out of 100. These extremes give us what can be thought of as a 'reasonable' range within a given probability, as shown in Figure 5.8.

But what if we need to be more accurate? In this case we simply use the fact that, if we take 2.5 standard deviations on either side of our estimate, then 99 times out of 100 we will guess right for the range within which the real mean falls.

To use this method you need to check how to calculate the standard error (the standard deviation of your sample), which depends on sample size. If your sample is 30 or greater, you can use the normal distribution to estimate the confidence limits. If you can only get a sample size of less than 30, then you need to resort to a variant distribution called the *t*-distribution. (It is skewed, and using it involves estimating the degrees of freedom of the sample.)

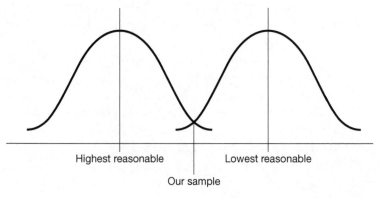

Highest reasonable   Lowest reasonable

Our sample

Figure 5.8
The Overlapping Normal Distributions of Confidence Limits

HYPOTHESIS TESTING

You must be able to detect changes that are taking place if you are ever going to answer a question of observation, and if you are predicting or planning it is even more important.

The problem with detecting change is that you cannot afford the time or the money to keep carrying out a complete census of your data set. You are going to have to take samples, and you know that every sample you take will be different.

You could end up basing a costly decision on the variation of one sample from another. You already know that the means of samples are normally distributed, so any results you get will be spread out. Under no circumstances do you expect two measures taken at different times from the same population to give exactly the same answer, but by how much is it reasonable for them to differ?

Fortunately you can again make use of Gauss's work here, because his theory of errors lets you answer that question. His Central Limit Theorem said that, if you keep taking samples from the same population, then 95 times out of 100 the mean value of the samples will all be within two standard errors of the mean. You can work out the standard error by adjusting the standard deviation of the sample for the sample size. So this gives you a way of checking if anything is changing, because it implies that if your samples have come from a different grouping, they will be further than two standard errors from the mean.

Hypothesis testing is a very useful technique because you need not use it just to see if there are differences between groups; you can also test the same group at different times and see if any changes are taking place. This trick is useful for both prediction problems in market research and for planning problems in quality control.

Hypothesis testing is a statistical way of choosing between two claims H_0 (which is the null hypothesis) and H_A (which is the alternative hypothesis). For example, your null hypothesis could be that the mean of a set of observations of the average number of tins of baked beans purchased per month by a group of customers was unchanged when a price promotion deal was introduced. Your alternative hypothesis could be the price changed the mean number of sales. If you can reject the hypothesis that there was no change, then you can conclude there *was* a change – which was what you were interested in testing.

When you select an hypothesis you can make an error. The possible errors are called Type I and Type II. A Type I error occurs when you select H_A by mistake, instead of selecting H_0. A Type II error occurs when you select H_0 by mistake, instead of selecting H_A. The probability of a Type I error is called the 'Level of test'; the probability of a Type II error is hard to determine, since it depends on what has to be an unknown parameter.

If you pose a question which needs hypothesis testing to provide evidence of an answer, be careful when formulating your null and alternative hypothesis to try to minimize both Type I and Type II errors. The two types of errors are inversely related, which means there is always going to be a trade-off of risk between them. The smaller you make the risk of one, the larger the risk of the other becomes. But then there is never such a thing as a free lunch!

One of the most important limitations to realize about statistics is that it is totally unable to prove anything at all. It can only *fail* to prove something. If you want to know if something might be true, you have to try and prove the opposite. If you fail, then you can say that the opposite is likely. You still don't know if it is true, but you can be a lot more comfortable saying that it might well be. Statisticians call this way of doing things 'setting up a null hypothesis'. An hypothesis is an idea that you want to test. If you set up two conflicting ones, then one must be rejected. You then know that the other one must be reasonable, although you cannot say you have proved it – you can only say you failed to disprove it.

HOW TO TEST FOR RELATIONSHIPS

Many problems of observation will demand that you can show that what you have observed is a good representation of reality. Often your data sets will be categorical data, rather than numerical. You may be trying to show, say, that the firm you are studying is not implementing policies that lead to sexual discrimination. Your data set will consist of counts of the numbers of males and females in different situations. Your problem is to show that there is no bias in the way the ratio of the sexes is distributed across the various situations. To do this you have to show that the observed distribution of the sex ratio is within the limits of expected variation due to chance, if the ratio was randomly distributed (as it will be if there is no sexual bias).

This is the sort of question where you need to show that there is no relationship between sexual discrimination and the distribution of jobs. But other relationship problems concern showing that a relationship really does exist: for example, that a certain group of customers really do prefer Brand X to Brand Y. Let's start by looking at the problem of goodness of fit and independence.

Goodness of fit and independence

This is a type of hypothesis test, where you test whether the data 'fits' a particular distribution or not. This can be a probability distribution or, as in the case of sexual discrimination, a random distribution. You use a chi-square test (meaning the probability distribution for the hypothesis test is χ^2) to determine if there is a fit or not. The null and the alternate hypotheses for this test may be written in sentences or may be stated as equations or inequalities.

You have calculated the difference between the expected values and the observed values, which gives you the value of a test statistic, which can be looked up on chi-square distribution to see which hypothesis you choose. This will allow you either to accept or reject your null hypotheses. If you are looking for bias, your null hypotheses should be of the form 'My data set is randomly distributed', because rejecting the null hypothesis says there has to be bias of some sort. Or it could be 'My data set is a normal/binomial/Poisson distribution', so allowing you to reject that possibility. You might well use this test to see if you can validly apply a particular statistical model to your problem.

A goodness-of-fit test is almost always right-tailed. If the observed values and the corresponding expected values are not close to each other, then the test statistic can get very large and will be way out in the right tail of the chi-square curve.

Correlation and regression

Correlation is a technique you can use to describe an observed relationship between instances of two events. A systematic pattern will be seen in events that are correlated. When the events involve numbers, a positive correlation means that as one increases, the other increases as well. A negative correlation means that as one increases, the other decreases. Remember, however, that a high degree of correlation does not imply causation. Just because two events are correlated does not mean that one is causing the other, or has anything to do with it. Correlations deal only with observed instances of events, and you can not infer causal conclusions from correlation evidence alone. Strong correlation, however, does often warrant further investigation to determine causation, and if you can also show a chain of sequential actions leading to the correlation, this can make a strong case. Items which move closely together have a correlation of 1, or –1, while items which move entirely independently of each other have a correlation of 0.

Regression is a process of mapping a trend line (usually of the form $y = m^*x + c$ (although other polynomials, logarithmic or exponential curves may be used), as already discussed. The method works by choosing a freely moving curve which minimizes the square of the errors of the fit – hence it is often called the Method of Least Square. Both Excel and SPSS have correlation and regression packages within them.

This chapter has given you a quick overview of what is possible within the discipline of statistics. If you need to use any of these techniques the detailed methods of application can be found in any good textbook[4] or by using the help and tutorial systems to be found in Excel (http://office.microsoft.com/en-gb/training/CR100479681033.aspx) and built into SPSS.

---

4   Suitable textbooks are: Buglear, John (2010) *Stats Means Business: A guide to business statistics*, Oxford, Butterworth-Heinemann. Urdan, Timothy (2010) *Statistics in Plain English*, Oxford, Routledge. Davies, Glyn & Pecar, Branko (2010) *Business Statistics Using Excel*, Oxford, OUP.

GROUP DISCUSSION TOPIC FOR CHAPTER 5

Spend an hour or two investigating the help and tutorial systems of Excel, SPSS or Minitab (whichever packages are available in your university computer labs) before meeting with your study group. If you are unfamiliar with these packages, work through the online tutorials which are built into their help systems.

Return to your written assignment for Chapter 1 and identify how you can record, analyse and present the data which you decided you will need in order to answer your question.

Take notes on the discussion to add to your Learning Log.

Chapter

6

PLANNING YOUR RESEARCH PROJECT

HOW DO YOU KNOW THAT?

T HE KEY STEPS IN beginning a research project are:

1. Choose a suitable problem. This is a strategic decision and involves consideration of the demands of all the stakeholders.
2. Ask a sensible question. This is a tactical decision which involves making sure the scope of the necessary inquiry is suitable for the word count and time limit involved. Remember, a good trick is to phrase the question in the first person. E.g. 'How can I . . . ?'
3. Decide on the nature of the answer, bearing in mind the taxonomy of answers that I listed in Chapter 4.
4. Work out what data you need to provide the evidence for your answer and how you will collect it, store it, access it and analyse it.

THE USE OF EVIDENCE

We have already found that different questions require different evidence to demonstrate an acceptable answer. We have looked at the statistical tools we can use to display patterns within data sets, at the ways in which we can test if our observations and predictions fit reality, at how we can use time as a proxy variable to forecast outcomes, and how we can test for relationships and/or bias between events. The one thing we have not yet looked at is how to build up a complete set of observations in order to construct a case study.

As we have seen, there are two basic ways to create an answer to your question:

- to list an historical chain of events leading from the question to the answer, so demonstrating the inevitability of the outcome in the particular set of circumstances that applied;
- to develop an unchallengeable chain of logic that shows why your answer must be correct.

Whichever approach your question requires in order to be answered, though, your first step towards a successful dissertation has to be to write out a complete answer to the questions, showing all the evidence and its sources.

Metaphorically, you can think of this process as akin to building a river crossing by embedding stepping stones in a fast-flowing stream. Imagine that the question is on the bank where you are standing, and the answer on the far bank. Before you can reach the answer, you must collect a pile of large stones on your side of the river. (This is your evidence, and will be stored in a Word Outline, where you can sort it and keep it linked to its sources.) Next you will have to place the stones across the torrent in a line stretching from the question to the answer. They will not all be the same size, and the water will not always be the same depth, so your problem is to place the stones in the water in such a way that:

- the top of each stone is clear of the water, so you do not get your feet wet when you stand on it (that is to say, your evidence should prove the point that needs proving to establish that step in the argument);
- the sequence of stones is so placed that you can step easily from one to the next without overextending yourself, slipping into the water and being swept away from the answer (that is to say, your chain of evidence should follow logically and inevitably from one point to the next, with no chance of your reader getting lost on the way).

As you try to do this, you may find that either your stones are not big enough to project above the water (i.e. your evidence is not strong enough), or you don't have enough stones (your chain of evidence is not sufficient to sustain your reasoning). You will only discover these difficulties when you try to write the first draft of your dissertation.

I will return to this problem later, but my advice is to start writing as soon as you possibly can, otherwise you could lull yourself into a false sense of security when you are simply thinking about the writing of your dissertation. At that stage your ideas will seem wonderful and complete as they hover in your mind. It is only when you try committing them to the blank page that they can dissolve into diaphanous fairy dust, and the vast areas of missing logic or evidence start to become apparent.

To see how you get this process under way let us look at the practicalities of the two ways of collecting your pile of stones.

BUILDING AN HISTORICAL SEQUENCE USING DATED EVENTS

The main issue with case-study-type answers is to decide what happened and when it happened. To establish a chain of cause and effect you need to understand the sequence of events. If the object of your interest has not been studied before, then you may well find that the information you need is scattered over a number of sources. Typical sources for the study of business scenarios would be:

- newspaper articles;
- dated memos and emails;
- recollections about particular events collected by interview;
- internal company press releases and newsletters;
- company accounts and reports;
- legal documents (perhaps showing dates of mergers or sales, etc.);
- published accounts of the events in memoirs or textbooks;
- business blogs and online comment.

Your problem with such a disparate mix of sources is to conflate them into a sequence that makes sense of what happened.

A useful technique for analysing this type of data is to use the sorting function in an Excel spreadsheet to create a time-line.

As an example of how this method works, let me show you how I used it to piece together the role Sir Robert Moray played in the events that led up to the foundation of the Royal Society in 1640.

Each time I found an interesting event connected with Moray (mainly from his contemporaries' diaries) I entered it into a spreadsheet. I put in as much of the date of the event as I had: year, month and day if possible. I then sorted the list by year, month and day, so that the events, from whatever source I had obtained them, were sequenced in the order they happened. From such a detailed time-line I was able to build up a picture of the events, and eventually deduced what happened. The result was a time-sequence table, such as the example section shown in Table 6.1.

In an adjacent column of the spreadsheet I stored the reference source from which I obtained the information about the event and its dating. Then, when I came to write up the narrative of the events, I could footnote the reference for each individual happening. Table 6.2 illustrates another part of this time-line, showing the reference sources I used for each of these events.

This technique is an extremely useful way of helping you avoid getting bogged down in detail. When you come across a pertinent event you can summarize it, add it into the bottom line of your time-line (along with its reference source) and then re-sort the time-line to show the event in its correct place in the historical sequence of your case study.

This sorted time-line is extremely helpful when you attempt to write a first draft of the event and consequence sequence.

BUILDING A CHAIN OF LOGIC

If your question is such that it needs to be answered by building a chain of logic, then you need to consider exactly how to forge that chain. Usually you will need to select, then consult, a particular model or piece of business theory. (This means first looking at the literature to make sure you understand the theory or model, next citing the sources from which it was drawn, and then stating the assumptions

Table 6.1
Creating a Time-line

Year	Month	Day	Event
1660	5	26	Charles II returns to London
1660	8	17	William Moray, Robert's younger brother appointed Master of Works and General Warden of Masons in Scotland
1660	11	28	Royal Society formally constituted at Gresham College
1661	2		Robert Moray reappointed Privy Counsellor to Charles II
1661	10	16	Robert Moray thanks Charles II in person for the Royal Charter for the Society
1662	5	20	Charles II marries Catherine of Braganza
1662	7	15	First Charter Granted to Royal Society
1662	8	13	Royal Society thanks Robert Moray for his help in obtaining Royal Charter
1662	10		Charles II grants RS funds
1663	3		Robert Moray plans demonstration experiments for Charles II's visit to Royal Society
1663	4	15	Robert Moray plans a survey of the stars of the Zodiac by Members of the Royal Society
1663	4	22	Second Charter Granted to Royal Society
1663	7		Robert Moray carries out experiments for Charles II
1665	11		Robert Moray notes in letter that he has completed 24 pages of his History of Freemasonry
1665			Sir Robert Moray starts to write a history of Freemasonry
1666			Sir Robert Moray writes to John Evelyn 'It seems you conclude me a greater master in another sort of Philosophy than the RS'
1667			Robert Moray goes to Scotland as Charles II's commissioner
1669			Sir William Moray resigns as General Warden of Scotland
1670	8		Charles II uses Masonic identification to Moray at Windsor
1670			Robert Moray quarrels with Lauderdale
1672			England at war with Netherlands
1673	7	4	Robert Moray dies
1673	7	6	Robert Moray buried in Westminster Abbey

which underpin its implementation in your case.) Your first step is to show that the theory, or model, applies to the problem you have chosen, and so can be used to provide evidence which throws light on the issue. Your second step is show that the question you have asked can be answered using the type of evidence that the model, or theory, can reveal.

Table 6.2
Inserting Sources in a Time-line

Year	Event	Source
1598	First Schaw Statutes	SOF, p. 80, Word file
1598	Schaw becomes General Warden of the Masons of Scotland	IC, p. 92
1599	Second Schaw Statutes	SOF, p. 81, Word file
1599	Oldest minutes from Edinburgh Lodge	SOF, p. 103, Word file
1600	Lodge of Glasgow formed	SOF, p. 120, Word file
1601	First St Clair Charter	SOF, p. 85, Word file
1601	John Mylne is Warden of Lodge of Scoon and Perth when it initiates King James VI	SOF, p. 118, Word file
1613	Lodge of Glasgow mentioned in minutes of Incorporation	SOF, p. 120, Word file
1617	William the Wastrel flees to Ireland; succeeded by his son William who employed Masons to rebuild Roslin Castle	Origins, p. 57
1628	Second St Clair Charter	SOF, p. 86, Word file
1641	Sir Robert Moray initiated in Newcastle by Lodge of Edinburgh	SOF, p. 127, Word file
1642	Oldest Minutes from Kilwinning	SOF, p. 96, Word file
1658	Lodge of Scoon and Perth records Kilwinning legend in minutes	SOF, p. 117, Word file
1670	Laws and Statutes of the Lodge of Aberdeen recorded	SOF, p. 136, Word file
1677	Kilwinning Charters a lodge in Edinburgh	SOF, p. 100, Word file
1677	Mother Killwinning consecrates first daughter Lodge Cannongate Kilwinning in Edinburgh	SOF, p. 115, Word file
1678	Lodge Old Kilwinning St John formed in Inverness	SOF, p. 122, Word file
1683	Lodge of Edinburgh stops adding to the weapons store and accepts money in lieu of implements of warfare	SOF, p. 110, Word file
1688	Edinburgh lodge creates daughter lodge of Leith and Canongate	SOF, p. 121, Word file

Once you have proved the validity of your approach you must collect data that can then be processed by the model to create evidence for your answer. Often you will need the statistical techniques of data sorting, presentation and pattern detection that we have looked at above. For more technical issues you may also to need to draw on regression, curve-fitting and correlation to show links (although you need to remember that correlation does not prove a cause, only that data movements happen together). In a few cases you may need to set up a statistical hypothesis and then test it against your observations.

I would suggest the best way to identify what is needed for your particular project is to draw up a flow chart of actions, and to make sure that you can see the necessary sequence for each of them, so that each step feeds into the next and eventually supports the final result.

PLANNING YOUR WORK

Once you have listed all the tasks you need to complete, you must do one of two things:

- reveal, or invent, your answer (which you do depends on your choice of problem and question);
- collect the evidence ready to prove its correctness.

At this stage you should produce a plan of work for the dissertation. I would suggest producing a Gantt chart of the events, keeping an eye out for the critical path, the deadlines for submission and any periods where your day job, personal life or other academic work commitments may leave you unable to devote time to the project. Be realistic in the targets you set, and take note that when you have created the first draft of your complete answer, it will still be a long way from being a finished dissertation. Set yourself milestones, which you can agree with your supervisor.

Typical milestones are:

1. to choose and justify your choice of problem;
2. to propose a question which satisfies all stakeholders;
3. to list the types and sources of data needed to provide an answer;
4. to complete your primary/secondary data collection;
5. to complete your study of the models or theory you intend to use, and to justify your choice;
6. to be ready to create a complete answer to your question, with evidence for each step in the chain;
7. to write a first draft;
8. to defend the first draft to your supervisor or a trusted critical friend.

Getting to a first draft

Not until you try to write out a full account of your question, and its answer, will you find out if there are any gaps in your justification. I would suggest you plan to complete a first draft as soon as you can, because attempting (and failing) to write it usually reveals the things which got overlooked in your initial plan, and which may well force you to go back to collect more data – or even make you reconsider your choice of model, or if your question is actually capable of being answered.

Many students defer the writing stage by burying themselves in a welter of procrastination and untested activity, which they mistake for progress. But, until you try to write out your argument, it always seems far better than it really is. Draft it out and then set it aside for a while; return to it a few days later, and you will see its faults with a clearer eye. This is the point at which you often need to go back to your plan and reconsider what you are trying to do. (You may even need to revise your question to make it manageable within the constraints of time and word count.)

When you write the first draft don't worry about the word count, grammar or layout – all these can be dealt with in later drafts. It is always easier to cut long writing than to have to provide extra material, and it is usually easier to improve something already written than to write it in the first place. The only purpose of the first draft is to be complete: it should provide a full and comprehensive answer to your question with all the supporting evidence that any neutral observer could ask for.

The best way to test your first draft is to tell it verbally to your supervisor and see if s/he understands and accepts your answer. Ask them to question you if anything is not clear, and take careful note of where they fail to understand as you try to explain your points. It is important to realize that during this defence process the reader of the report can seek clarification if they don't understand. Once the report is finalized, though, all a reader can do is try to make sense of what you have written down. Then, if you have failed to explain something or have missed out a step, your reader will be lost and could well end up dismissing your whole thesis.

You should ask your tutor or critical friend to act as an intelligent but ignorant observer. If anything is not clear encourage them to ask for an explanation, and keep questioning until the matter is completely explained. (When you are close to a topic you often take for granted many things that someone fresh to the topic does not understand – or, even worse, thinks they do understand when in fact have got the concept totally confused.)

If you can defend your answer and support all your evidence from this draft, then you are ready to move to the next stages of dissertation writing, which I will discuss in the next chapter.

GROUP DISCUSSION TOPIC FOR CHAPTER 6

Using the problems, questions, evidence needs, data collection and proposed analysis techniques you have decided upon, produce flow charts and suitable milestones for your problem.

If you have a reasonable-sized study group of students who are all at the same stage, you should have a range of different problems between you. Be prepared to comment on the differences between your individual problems in terms of how difficult they were to flow-chart and how the milestones varied. Note the results in your Learning Log.

Finally use the notes in your Learning Log to write your own dissertation proposal and research plan.

7

CREATING A NARRATIVE THREAD FOR YOUR DISSERTATION

THE SERIOUS BUSINESS OF FAIRY STORIES

A COMMON DIFFICULTY for most postgraduate students is how to approach the mechanics of writing up the dissertation. It may be the longest document you have tackled – sometimes it seems like a small book – and so rather beyond your previous writing experience. You can end up writing a list of 'things I did' to fill the space, or (even worse) populating a template for a Science A-level Laboratory Report, with randomly ordered facts and figures. (Whenever I see a dissertation containing a chapter headed 'Literature Survey', I know it will show little understanding of how to communicate enthusiasm for a set of research findings.) But writing is a craft, and it can be taught. This chapter describes how you can study the process and learn the craft.

Understanding how a myth works also helps you present your research findings in a logical and readable way. A myth is not simply a fanciful ramble: the most powerful myths contain Truths that have been made easier to grasp by hiding them within a 'good story'. So I am going to set you an odd piece of homework, but one that will help you learn to present a detailed technical argument – I want you to read fairy stories.

The reason is simple. As children we all listen to fairy stories, and when we are told a new story it increases the accumulated experience of all the previous stories we have heard. We quickly develop expectations of what is going to happen, and initially we revise our expectations as the story unfolds. As long as the story fits one of the early templates burned into our childhood minds, then we are comfortable with how it develops, even if we are surprised by the new detail it contains. But if none of our templates fits the developing story, then we start to become disappointed and may even begin to distrust the account we are given, feeling 'that doesn't seem right!' without really knowing why.

Think of the first fairy story you remember being told, and also of your favourite story. The speed with which you can recall them shows you how embedded these stories are in your mind. These traditional fairy stories you learned as a child can be used as a scaffolding on which to erect a reasonable narrative thread for telling the business story your dissertation has researched. State the question you have posed for your research and the answer you have discovered and look for the most appropriate fairy scaffolding to link the two. You need to explore how to tell the story of your journey from the question to the answer by means of a traditional fairy story which closely corresponds to that journey. You can do this by creating a storyboard, using the outline of your chosen fairy story. Look how each character serves a purpose in revealing the story, and look at the order in which they all appear. Next you must think about your business story. Who is the handsome prince, who the beautiful princess and who the wicked villain. Alongside the storyboard of the fairy story, create the parallel business story. Decide which participants in the business story are to play what fairy-tale character. Then introduce them, the information they contribute and actions they carry out in the order their fairy prototypes appeared and acted in the fairy template. In this way your business story will follow the rules of story-telling which are burned into everybody's brains from childhood. Once you have established the roles and sequences of a storyboard for your business story, using the well-tried template of an acceptable fairy story, then you can dispense with the fairy scaffolding and concentrate on telling a compelling business story, making sure you support the actions in your narrative with suitable business theory and strong evidence.

I believe that one of the major spurs to the evolution of the human mind is our ability to tell stories. And along with this goes the use of metaphor – which helps to explain complex things that we find hard to understand in terms of simpler things that we can visualize. In this way we can transmit knowledge to members of the next generation without their having to learn everything anew from personal experience. This human ability lies at the heart of the advance of civilization. As Steven Pinker puts it:

> You and I belong to a species with a remarkable ability: we can shape events in each other's brains with exquisite precision. I am not referring to telepathy or mind control or the other obsessions of fringe science; even in the depictions of believers these are blunt instruments compared to an ability that is uncontroversially present in every one of us. That ability is language. Simply by making noises with our mouths, we can reliably cause precise new combinations of ideas to arise in each other's minds. The ability comes so naturally that we are apt to forget what a miracle it is.
>
> (Pinker 1994)

Scientists since the time of Newton have used mathematical reasoning to help them understand the universe. Nobel prize winner in physics Richard Feynman comments:

> If you are interested in the ultimate character of the physical world . . . our only way to understand that is through a mathematical type of reasoning. . . . I don't think a person can fully appreciate . . . these particular aspects of the world . . . without an understanding of mathematics . . . there are many, many aspects of the world that mathematics is unnecessary for, such as love . . . [but to] not know mathematics is a severe limitation in understanding the world.
>
> (Feynman 2007)

But this highly skilled scientist uses the power of myth, and the insight of metaphor to help him visualize the way forward. The mathematics come after the insight and justify it. He explains how he developed his way of using stories to teach and to help to understand the world.

> I got a kick, when I was a boy, out of my father telling me things, so I tried to tell my son things that were interesting about the

world. When he was very small we used to rock him to bed, you know, and tell him stories, and I'd make up a story about little people that were about so high who would walk along and they would go on picnics and so on, and they lived in the ventilator; and they'd go through these woods which had great big long tall blue things like trees, but without leaves and only one stalk, and they had to walk between them and so on; and he'd gradually catch on that that was the rug, the nap of the rug, the blue rug, and he loved this game because I would describe all these things from an odd point of view and he liked to hear the stories, and we got all kinds of wonderful things – he even went to a moist cave where the wind kept going in and out – it was coming in cool and went out warm and so on. It was inside the dog's nose that they went, and then of course I could tell him all about physiology by this way and so on. He loved that, and so I told him lots of stuff, and I enjoyed it because I was telling him stuff that I liked, and we had fun when he would guess what it was and so on.

Nonetheless, although he saw stories as a good way of teaching, he went on to say:

> It is probable that the human mind evolved from that of an animal; and it evolved in a certain way such that it is like any new tool, in that it has its diseases and difficulties . . . one of the troubles is that it gets polluted by its own superstitions, it confuses itself.

The power of a story can take hold of a person's mind and be so convincing that it sounds as if it simply must be correct. For many years the Church believed, and taught, the myth that the sun went round the earth, because it was such a convincing story. When Galileo invented the telescope and found this wasn't true, the myth was stronger than the science, and Galileo was made to state publicly his belief in the myth he had just disproved. In this case the story was stronger than the Truth, and it served the Church's political purposes better.

THE POWER OF MYTH

Sometimes thinking in terms of myth and metaphor can bring about change. Einstein told how he was introduced to Aaron Bernstein's popular books on natural science. His biographer, physicist Michio Kaku, reported him as saying:

> that it was 'a work which I read with breathless attention'. This book would have a fateful impact on him, because the author included a discussion on the mysteries of electricity. Bernstein asked the reader to take a fanciful ride inside a telegraph wire, racing alongside an electric signal at fantastic speeds.
>
> At the age of sixteen, Einstein had a daydream that led him to an insight which would later change the course of human history. Perhaps remembering the fanciful ride taken in Bernstein's book, Einstein imagined himself running alongside a light beam and asked himself a fateful question: What would the light beam look like? Like Newton visualizing throwing a rock until it orbited the earth like the moon, Einstein's attempt to imagine such a light beam would yield deep and surprising results.
>
> (Kaku 2004)

There is a substantial body of current research literature looking at the use of myth as a tool for understanding business. This type of analysis of how stories work has a long history. In the introduction to *Poetics* our old friend Aristotle, writing in 350 BCE, said:

> I propose to treat of Poetry in itself and of its various kinds, noting the essential quality of each, to inquire into the structure of the plot as requisite to a good poem; into the number and nature of the parts of which a poem is composed; and similarly into whatever else falls within the same inquiry. Following, then, the order of nature, let us begin with the principles which come first.
>
> (http://classics.mit.edu/Aristotle/poetics.1.1.html)

This was the first real study of how structure is inevitable in successful story-telling. He analysed the craft of the poet as that of a teller of stories which inspire the human spirit and which are of universal and timeless interest.

> It is not the function of the poet to relate what has happened, but what may happen – what is possible according to the law of probability or necessity. The poet and the historian differ not by writing in verse or in prose. The work of Herodotus might be put into verse, and it would still be a species of history, with meter no less than without it. The true difference is that one relates what has happened, the other what may happen. Poetry, therefore, is a more philosophical and a higher thing than history: for poetry tends to express the universal, history the particular. By the universal I mean how a person of a certain type can on occasion speak or act according to the law of probability or necessity; and it is this universality at which poetry aims.

When anybody writes a story or retells myth, there are a limited number of logical alternatives; some are generally interesting, others are not. Conflict between strangers is of little interest because it is a natural part of human nature, he observes. But conflict between people who we feel should love each other intrigues us. A mother who thanks God that it is her son, rather than her lover who has been killed is a deep subject for a story, as Henry James showed. The drama of the situation forces us to turn the next page to see what will happen next. This is the art of the soap-opera writers, who are the natural successors to the dramatic analysis of Aristotle. This analysis leads him to develop a basic algorithm of dramatic relations, which he uses to produce a taxonomy of story-lines that exploit all the logical possibilities of a good story. He noticed that there are deep themes that fascinate all humans; these are the ingredients of the social life that makes us human.

Denis Dutton, the editor of the magazine *Philosophy and Literature*, said:

> The basic situations of fiction are a product of fundamental, hard-wired interests human beings have in love, death, adventure, family, justice, and adversity. These values counted as much in the Pleistocene as today, which is why they are so intensively

studied by evolutionary psychologists. Our fictions are populated with character-types relevant to these themes: beautiful young women, handsome strong men, courageous leaders, children needing protection, wise old people. Add to this the threats and obstacles to the fulfillment of love and fortune, including both bad luck and villains, and you have the makings of literature. Story plots are not unconscious archetypes, but follow, as Aristotle realized, from human interests and the logic of what is possible.

(Dutton 2005)

In 2004 literary critic Christopher Booker, a founding editor of *Private Eye*, wrote an analysis of the seven main themes in fiction, and I found that he had articulated the main fairy-tale motifs which had been making regular appearances in my students' listings of their favourites. The seven basic stories which my students report are:

1. Killing the Monster (Jack and the Beanstalk).
2. The Quest (King Arthur and the Search for the Holy Grail).
3. Voyage and Return (Robinson Crusoe).
4. Rags to Riches (Cinderella).
5. Death and Resurrection (Snow White).
6. Comedy (Jeeves and Wooster).
7. Tragedy (Hamlet).

The last two items on this list are much broader categories than the first five. They could almost be considered as *genres* of writing, and hence each could have its own list of themes, but this is beyond the scope of this little book. Also, I have not come across many successful applications of the tragedy and comedy themes to business writing; it is the first five categories that are most useful as aids to dissertation writing.

Every successful story ever told uses combinations and blends of these basic stories. Booker makes this point in the introduction to his detailed analysis of story-telling.

We spend a phenomenal amount of our lives following stories: telling them; listening to them; reading them; watching them being acted out on the television screen or in films or on a stage. They are far and away one of the most important features of our everyday existence. . . . Not only do fictional stories play such a significant role in our lives, as novels or plays, films or operas, comic strips or TV soaps. Through newspapers or television, our news is presented to us in the form of stories. Our history books are largely made up of stories. Even much of our conversation is taken up with recounting the events of everyday life in the form of stories. These structured sequences of imagery are in fact the most natural way we know to describe almost everything which happens in our lives.

(Booker 2004)

The interesting implication of the existence of these basic plots, which Booker has shown are endemic throughout human society, is that everybody identifies with the mythical structure as these stories unfold.

These patterns serve a far deeper and more significant purpose in our lives than we have realized . . . wherever men and women have told stories, all over the world, the stories emerging to their imaginations have tended to take shape in remarkably similar ways.

From the research I had carried out for my book *Turning the Hiram Key* I was already aware of the importance of story-telling in forming a sense of self-identity.

Human beings like stories. When you offer to tell a young child a story she will clap her hands in anticipation of the joy it will bring her. She expects pleasure, she hopes for an experience to excite her imagination and transport her to emotional places she will enjoy visiting. And this love of a good story stays with us humans throughout our lives. In fact, if I were asked to say how humans differ from other primate species I might try suggesting we are the only species to tell each other stories. . . . The myths that groups of people create define their society's values and beliefs. And those myths can long outlast the people who first tell them.

(Lomas 2005)

Since writing that, I have become even more convinced that myths speak to people at a level which takes no account of reality.

Story-telling seems to be an innate artefact of the development of the self-awareness that has made us human. In many ways it works in our favour helping the species to share knowledge over generations and conditioning the young to listen to their elders. Richard Dawkins, Professor of the Public Understanding of Science, at Oxford University, has noted this effect.

> More than any other species, we survive by the accumulated experience of previous generations, and that experience needs to be passed on to children for their protection and well-being. Theoretically, children might learn from personal experience. . . . But there will be a selective advantage to child brains that possess the rule of thumb: believe, without question, whatever your grown-ups tell you.
>
> (Dawkins 2006)

Dawkins goes on to recount a story which made a great impression on him as a child. It follows one of the classic plots and also the rules of tragedy. It begins with a dream of perfection and ends with the death that all the listeners foresee as inevitable. Dawkins tells how this story struck his childish mind and became so indelibly imprinted that he still finds it horrifying almost half a century after hearing it.

> I have never forgotten a horrifying sermon, preached in my school chapel when I was little. Horrifying in retrospect, that is: at the time, my child brain accepted it in the spirit intended by the preacher. He told us a story of a squad of soldiers, drilling beside a railway line. At a critical moment the drill sergeant's attention was distracted, and he failed to give the order to halt. The soldiers were so well schooled to obey orders without question that they carried on marching, right into the path of an oncoming train. Now, of course, I don't believe the story and I hope the preacher

didn't either. But I believed it when I was nine, because I heard it from an adult in authority over me. And whether he believed it or not, the preacher wished us children to admire and model ourselves on the soldiers' slavish and unquestioning obedience to an order, however preposterous, from an authority figure. Speaking for myself, I think we did admire it. As an adult I find it almost impossible to credit that my childhood self wondered whether I would have had the courage to do my duty by marching under the train. But that, for what it is worth, is how I remember my feelings. The sermon obviously made a deep impression on me, for I have remembered it and passed it on to you.

This shows the lingering power that a story has even on the adult mind of man noted for his rational and scientific thinking. Just imagine, then, what impact powerful myths can have on a business audience.

The use of a narrative template to create a logical and persuasive business case is a writing skill that can be taught. It draws on the innate knowledge absorbed by all children as they learn their own mother tongue by listening to stories. By telling the child within our audience a story that is familiar, we can present new material in a way that makes it both acceptable and believable.

I have come to believe that the ancient art of story-telling is a powerful technique for managers, to make them better communicators, and hence better leaders, and part of my motive for writing this little book is to share that idea more widely with students who want to learn how to write well.

The best way to understand the structure of the seven basic plots is to read them in their simplest form as children's fairy stories. If you can read the stories out loud to your own children, or to nieces or nephews, then you will see at first hand just how enthralling these basic stories are, and how young children love them, learn them and will recall them for the rest of their lives. Remember, every reader of your dissertation, business report or sales pitch was once a story-loving child, and if you can enthral your reader's inner child they will enjoy reading your work and be predisposed to accept your arguments and proposals.

APPLYING NARRATIVE STRUCTURE TO
BUSINESS WRITING

A well crafted piece of writing has to go through at least three drafts. Each draft serves a separate purpose, and none of the tasks involved overlap. (It is, of course, quite possible that you may choose to write more than a single version of each draft.) This method of writing is the quickest way to produce an acceptable dissertation, as it avoids waste and repetition.

The three stages are:

1. *Research* and gathering information and evidence to answer your question (Draft 1).
2. *Structuring* the narrative thread of your answer (Draft 2).
3. *Editing* and final presentation of the text (Draft 3).

I suggest when you draw up a time plan for the delivery of each draft that you allow a minimum of four weeks for the final two drafting processes.

To prepare yourself, first explain to your trusted critical friend the question you are setting out to answer. This should not be a formal academic statement of intent, which is often swathed in jargon and buried under mounds of statements in the passive voice. Put the question in the first person – for example:

'How can I understand and explain the factors which caused the collapse of GM Europe?'
'How can I produce a plan to optimize the marketing of Sun's new smartcard-based terminal client configuration software?'

Framing the question in these personal terms gives you a clearer idea of what you have to do.

Draft 1

Once you are sure of your question and have agreed it with your tutor, then set out to discover as much information as you need to be able to draft out a complete answer to it. When you have done that, and written up the material in chronological sequence, you have Draft 1. At this stage don't worry about style or word count – just completeness.

This will be the first time that you will attempt to put together a complete and logical exposition of the answer to your question. The process of writing will help you clarify your thoughts to a surprising extent. Before you try to write down your answer it will seem to be clear and complete, but once you try to write it down you will begin to realize that there are parts of the argument you don't quite understand. This stage of writing is important.

When you are ready to begin to write your first draft you will probably find you have a pile of material of differing degrees of usefulness. Sort it into three categories:

1.   Useful mainstream material.
2.   Material which is vaguely useful for backing up statements but not essential.
3.   Interesting but irrelevant material.

You need to include anything in the first category; you need to consider if you have space for things from the second; and data from the third category you ignore (no matter how much you enjoyed collecting it and writing it up!).

Start by clearly stating your question and explaining why it matters. Then answer your question fully and completely, showing each step of your evidence that leads you to your answer.

If you get stuck writing Draft 1 and can't get to an answer, I suggest you rethink the question. Until the first draft is complete, you are in charge of both the question and its answer. You may have answered a different question from the one you set out to study. If this happens then consider if you should change your question to the one you have actually answered. Or you may find that it is impossible to answer your original question. If this happens you may have to consider addressing a different, more reasonable, question.

Once you have written a complete first draft you are ready to defend it in a quick *viva* (and make sure your tutor or critical friend insists on seeing your supporting written material). You must satisfy them that you can give an acceptable answer to your question, and that your answer is fully supported by sound evidence. And, if they are not satisfied, you need to go away and get more data.

Only when you have managed to write a completely evidenced answer and defend it successfully do you move on to Draft 2.

Draft 2

I use a metaphor I introduced in the previous chapter to explain this part of the process. When you write a dissertation you take responsibility for guiding your reader from your question to your answer. If you imagine your research to be a large pile of stones heaped alongside a swift-flowing river, your job as a writer is take those stones and lodge them in the river to form stepping stones. Each step must be exactly where your reader needs to place their foot in order to cross safely. If there are too few stones, the reader will never reach the far bank. If they are not spaced correctly, the reader will fall in and be swept away (and, if you try to create more than one path across the river, they may hesitate over where to step and overbalance, with the same result). Only if enough stones of the right size are positioned the right distances apart can you hope to get your reader safely across the flood of confusion and unknowing that separates your question from your answer.

To lay out the sequence of stones, you need a plan which meets the readers' expectations of the necessary sequence and distance between stones. This is where fairy stories come in. You need to study how to tell the reader a story which leads from question to answer in the sort of logical sequence they are expecting. Study the sequence and development of the seven main story types and decide what story your data are telling. Then create a storyboard for the chosen story, showing the order of telling, the sequence of events and the roles played by each character. If it is a rags-to-riches story, a struggling UK manufacturer may be Cinderella, a foreign government offering loans to its own national consortiums may be the over-powering King forcing a marriage on his reluctant son; and potential consortiums of buyers would be the Ugly Sisters fighting over the prince – who in this case might well be the UK Department for Business, Enterprise and Regulatory Reform, who could make or break the deal.

What starts out as a list can soon become a gripping tale of business options and choices. The key is to choose a story that conveys the business insight the research has revealed, and then to draw on the reader's expectations of how a story should develop to make the outcome inevitable. In this way you can create a powerful business narrative, which generates in your reader the desired belief in your argument.

Once you have chosen a suitable fairy-story template, you need to draw up two parallel storyboards: one the fairy scaffolding, the other the business meat. Once this process is complete the fairy scaffolding is made to vanish, so that only the business narrative remains. (I do not even suggest you let your readers know you have been telling them a fairy-story – just let them enjoy the tale and accept the argument.) Constructing and testing this narrative thread is the work of Draft 2.

Draft 3

The final step is to edit the text using the normal copy-editing techniques, which I shall summarize in Chapter 8. The language is polished, repetition is cut ruthlessly, the verbs are honed and tightened, all adjectives are killed on sight, references are checked and annotated clearly, and the textual widows and orphans reunited.

To sum up, here are the minimum number of stages a piece of writing needs to go through to have a hope of being acceptable.

Draft 1: Answer the question fully and defend it.
Draft 2: Structure the narrative thread to engage the reader and reorganize the material as required by the story line.
Draft 3: Work on language, layout and word count.

By the end of the process a dissertation emerges which meets the requirements of all three stakeholders: university, student and employer. In my experience, once you have been taught this method you will be able to apply it to all your writing, and you will become a much more effective communicator.

GROUP DISCUSSION TOPIC FOR CHAPTER 7

Once all your study group have written their First Drafts, arrange to meet and present your question and its provable answer to the group. Listen to any queries and answer any misunderstandings. Each of you should defend your First Draft to the rest of the group and then arrange to meet again when all the identified gaps or misunderstandings in the drafts have been dealt with. Once you are happy you can defend your answer, then choose the plot line that best fits the story you have created. Before you next meet draw up a storyboard showing who will play the fairy characters in your business narrative.

Present the storyboard to your study group and discuss it with them. Take notes on the feedback and then write up your final version of Draft 2 ready for copy-editing.

Chapter

8

THE MECHANICS OF WRITING

MAKE THE READING EASY

O NE OF THE MOST IMPORTANT skills you need to develop as a business professional is written communication. It is the most important step in the process of transferring information and influencing the actions of others. When you are writing up a dissertation it does not matter how good your research was, or how wonderful your findings, if you cannot express them clearly to others.

Effective and interesting writing requires that you know your reader and maintain a polite consideration for that reader's needs. Start by remembering that the readers of your dissertation can have different motives, and these motives can change. There are two main motives. A dissertation *reader* starts at the beginning, reads through to the end of the report. A dissertation *user* dips in and only reads bits which s/he thinks are likely to be useful. Remember, though, that once a reader gets to the end of the dissertation they then magically change into a dissertation user.

Dissertation users look at the beginning of the report, and after reading a few pages turn to the end and read the conclusions. They may then go to the contents page and select any bits that appear of particular interest to read in more detail. Remember, every dissertation *examiner* starts out as a reader, but, once the body of the work has been looked at, turns into a dissertation user as they reach their final assessment of a mark. Second markers (the academics who make sure your first marker has been fair) are dissertation users from the beginning, and company sponsors or library readers are also dissertation users from the start. It is worth noting that a user who has a good initial experience of a dissertation has the potential to become a reader.

Users will often not read the whole dissertation, and the sections they chose to read will not necessarily be read in the sequence in which you (the writer) wished to present them. Make sure your introductions and conclusions to each chapter can be read alone, without relying on other chapters which a user may not look at.

To make sure that you meet the potential needs of readers and users you should pay careful attention to helping them to find their way about your dissertation easily. The chapter titles shown in the table of contents should clearly indicate what the chapter is about. Subheadings should help the user find important points within the chapter and also assist the reader in following the unfolding of the plot. The conclusion of a chapter should summarize what you expect readers to take from it and alert them to what is coming in the next chapter. Then take care of users by summarizing in the opening of each chapter what it is going to cover; they may only read a single chapter, so each chapter should be virtually a freestanding essay, although when read in sequence the chapters should jointly tell a fuller and richer story.

There are simple polite devices which make life easier for all readers. For example, in each chapter when you first introduce an acronym spell it out: e.g. 'International Monetary Fund (IMF)'. You can then use it freely within that chapter. (If you use the acronym again three chapters later, though, it is polite to spell it out in full again in the first instance.) This avoids the reader having to break out of the story line to look up the acronym's meaning. Remember, your reader may not be as familiar with the jargon of your subject as you are – and anyway users dip into dissertations, and so may not have seen the section where you first introduced that 'obvious' acronym.

A user will decide what to read on the basis of what is needed most urgently and what is useful. It is therefore the writer's job to make sure the user's attention is drawn to the most important information, such as the conclusions and recommendations. The different sections of the dissertation must be clearly identified and logically placed, so that the overall pattern of the document is clear.

Whether you are writing a dissertation or a company report, it is vital that you identify your readership before you start to write.

Sometimes it is obvious – the first reader of your dissertation will be your supervisor, who is also your first examiner. However, in the case of a company report it might be a particular senior colleague (in this case someone you know), at other times it may be a member of a client organization (here the reader is identifiable but not personally known). The most daunting of all is a readership which consists of a range of people of differing interests and levels of expertise.

In the case of a dissertation, the examiner will have to take decisions on the basis of the information you have presented. So it is important to be clear about what your main readers want to know and how they will assess the information. (The motives of the various stakeholders in the dissertation were discussed in Chapter 2.) Thinking about motives and expectations is often helpful in getting the tone right – by which I mean making the dissertation accessible to, and assimilable by, the reader: understanding their point of view, organizing the material in a logical way and expressing it in a clear and accurate writing style with helpful well-drawn diagrams and tables of contents. It may also involve choosing a suitable method of binding and an easy-to-read typeface.

Good tone makes a reader want to read the report because it looks attractive – as opposed to putting them off because the physical process of reading looks as if it is going to be difficult.

WRITING STYLE AND READABILITY

As readers we are all sharply aware of the daily waste of words that results from poor writing. We suffer much, and heads buzz and eyes burn with trying to read material that has not been written clearly.

You must have had the experience of falling asleep over news or journal articles you really wanted to read. Their complexity can drug your concentration. And, unless you are a skilled mind-reader, you will have made mistakes because of the unclear writing of colleagues.

From experience as a reader I am opposed to:

- words that don't say what they mean;
- words that don't say anything;
- words that are merely used for display.

But do you ever look at your own writing from the point of view of your reader? Do you know how many different words and what sort of words your readers are likely to understand? Do you know what sort of words work best in transferring facts and ideas from reader to writer? Do you know what mixture of hard and easy words readers will tolerate, or what patterns and lengths of sentences they can handle without tiring? And what sort of writing is most likely to make your reader take action or hold their interest? Moreover, did you know that there is a simple way to measure your own writing against writing that has proved to be successful?

If you can answer all those questions correctly and use the knowledge in your writing, you are a rare and valuable human being. Most people don't even consider the questions, let alone the answers.

I have a golden rule when I write, which may also help you. It is: 'Write unto others as you would be written to'.

When sharing this idea with my students I break it down into Ten Commandments of Clear Writing.

1. If at all possible, keep your sentences short (and always remember to have a verb!).
2. Prefer the simple to the complex.
3. Prefer the familiar word to the unusual.
4. Avoid unnecessary words.
5. Put action into your verbs.
6. Write as you talk.
7. Use terms the reader can visualize.
8. Tie into your reader's experience.
9. Make full use of variety of style.
10. Write to *express*, not to *impress*.

If you want to know about readers, study their habits. It is not enough to ask, 'What can people read?' If someone's motive is strong enough they will plough through any complexity of words, signs or hieroglyphs. (I've seen my young son struggle through highly technical computer manuals which are atrociously written, because he wants to know something.) People can read the most complex material, given the incentive. But the material they *prefer* to read is written simply. Magazines, comics and newspapers are all regularly appearing publications that rely on their readers coming back for more. Make the reading hard and the readers don't come back.

So, what is it that people do read? Readability tests of best-selling books and popular magazines show that readers resist prose which requires more than Year 11 reading skills. You can test this by checking your own dissertation draft with the grammar-checker of any good word-processing program, which will assess it in terms of standard readability statistics. The most useful of these are the Gunning's Fog Index and Flesch–Kincaid Grade Level Index, both measuring readability in terms of the reading-age skills needed (roughly equivalent to the school year: an index of 11 is the reading skill of a typical Year 11 student). Another useful readability yardstick is the Flesch Reading Ease Score, which ranks the writing on a scale of 0–100, where 100 is extremely easy to read, and 0 is impossible.

The foregoing is not a condemnation of readers for not being prepared to work hard enough. (Established authors have become established because they are well aware that their readers deserve respect.) But any material can be improved by being judged against the yardstick of this easy-reading range. Most successful professional writers of this century use a style with an average complexity within the range of 6 to 12 (Flesch Reading Ease Score 60 or more).

On the other hand, much written material issued by business, industry, professional journals and student dissertation writers is above the danger line of reading difficulty. There is no good reason for this. If you follow the Ten Commandments of Clear Writing you can avoid unnecessary complexity and avoid the waste it causes. Try to remember that you should not inflict difficult ideas and difficult readability on your reader both at the same time. In highly technical sections you will have to compromise, but at least for introductions and conclusions make the effort to write simply and clearly.

In addition, when you write your dissertation you need to make sure you know the layout and font requirements of your university. And ensure that you follow the regulations fully.

Here is a short checklist of things to watch out for when preparing your various drafts.

- Why should a busy reader bother to read your dissertation and what do you expect them to take away from it?

- What does the reader know about this subject?
- What does the reader *want* to know about this subject?
- What action does the reader expect to take after reading your dissertation? (This varies, depending on whether the reader is the examiner or your sponsor.)
- What action do you *want* the reader to take after reading your dissertation?
- Why are you writing this particular dissertation for this particular reader?
- Within the time limits set down in your terms of reference, collect as many relevant facts as you can (see Chapter 3).

You should always end your dissertation with a set of recommendations or conclusions which answer the business question you posed in your introduction. Do not write the final draft of the introduction until know how you are going to end. There is no excuse for failing to answer the question you set, as you are in control of both the beginning and the ending.

COPY-EDITING

The second draft of your dissertation should have reorganized your essential material into a narrative thread which tells a good business story. While creating your narrative you will have cut and pasted whole sections of text and rearranged sequences to fit the order of introduction of key players in your story, so the flow of your writing will have become disjointed.

The first thing to do when writing your third and final draft is therefore to 'top-and-tail' the new chapter layouts. Write a clear introduction to each indicating what it will cover. Then make sure you have a continuity of tense and viewpoint throughout the chapter. End by summing up what you expect the reader to take from the chapter, and then link into the next chapter, so the reader is not surprised by what comes next. For example, finish your chapter with something like this:

In this chapter the history of XYZ Ltd has been presented, and its place within the world markets outlined. In the next chapter we will consider its major competitors.

Then open the next chapter with something along the lines of:

> Now we understand the background to XYZ and its markets, this chapter will review the position and interactions of its major competitors.

Your reader should never experience a Monty Python moment ('And Now For Something Completely Different!') when you start a new chapter. The conclusion of a chapter should make clear what you expect them to have taken from that chapter and should alert them to where you are taking the argument next. This simple device also helps users see what they are choosing to miss out when they dip into the middle of a dissertation or report.

Once you have worked through, tidying the flow of the story and making sure you have maintained narrative hooks between chapters, you need to look at the conclusions. Do your conclusions answer the question you set out to answer? If not, then either you need to make sure they do, or you need to change your question to the one that you have answered. Once you have a satisfactory conclusion, you can write your Introduction.

The purpose of the Introduction is to:

- convince your reader that your business question is interesting and actually matters;
- make them want to read on and learn the answer.

An example of how this can be done is illustrated by one student's Introduction to a dissertation about how Rolls-Royce could effectively manage the provision of legacy spares for aircraft engines. He used a powerful image which I paraphrase below.

> In February 2000, six months before the one-hundredth birthday of Her Majesty Queen Elizabeth the Queen Mother, the RAF Battle of Britain Flight engineers had a problem. The Rolls-Royce Merlin engine which powered the Spitfire, which along with a Hurricane and Lancaster make up the historic flight, had run in a big end. The crankshaft was damaged beyond repair and the

aircraft grounded. The flight was scheduled to carry out a fly-past over Buckingham Palace as part of the birthday celebrations. What was to be done? The engine was sixty years old and a totally obsolete piece of kit. Naturally the RAF called Rolls-Royce and ordered a new crankshaft for immediate delivery.

Now the pressure was on. Rolls-Royce had built a strong world brand which prides itself on the reliability of its aircraft engines. To have the Queen Mother's birthday celebrations marred by a failure of one of the Rolls-Royce engines which had won the Battle of Britain would give the brand massive publicity of the most unwelcome kind.

What did the company do? The engineering drawings for the crankshaft were on file, similar machine tools to those used during the war were still available in the Apprentice Training School, and there were skilled trainers who could operate them. Rolls-Royce made a new crankshaft, complete with a set of matching shell bearings, to present to the RAF as a mark of respect for the Queen Mother's role in the Battle of Britain. The reputation of the brand was secured, but only at enormous cost in time, money and resources.

There are thousands of elderly Rolls-Royce aero-engines in use around the world. Nobody really knows how many of each of the hundreds of types are still in use, but if they break, their owners, like the RAF, expect to be able to repair them. This dissertation will look at the issue of legacy spares for Rolls-Royce aero-engines and outline the options for the company.

As an Introduction this ticks many boxes. It is easy to read (it has a Flesch Reading Ease Score of 61), it draws on powerful visual images, first to show the problem and then to explain its consequences. It dramatically highlights the importance of the problem to the company, and it teases the reader to join the author on a quest to solve this fascinating problem. And all this has been done in under 350 words on the first page of the dissertation. The rest of the dissertation was just as well written, and the student went on to gain a distinction in his MBA.

HITTING THE WORD COUNT

Once the beginning and ending are acceptable, check your word count. If your draft is within the limits set by your university, then there is no problem. If, as most students' second drafts are, it is over length, then you need to cut. The rule is simple: cut the least important sentence in the dissertation first. Then cut the next least important sentence. Keep doing this till you have got within 10 per cent of the word count limit (the rest will be cut when you work on your style). Word counts are imposed on dissertations to make sure that students can write an accurate and concise account of a piece of business research, so there is no excuse for going over the word limit. That simply shows an inability to judge what is important when communicating. Moreover, to submit a piece of writing that exceeds the word count not only shows no interest in helping a busy reader gain information, it betrays a sense of self-aggrandizement and self-indulgence.

Once you have your narrative flow established and your word count nearly under control, you should turn to your writing style. Your first job cut out flab. All initial drafts tend to be flabby. You often have an idea, write it down and then repeat it in a clearer form; the flab is the first attempt, which is often just left in place. Look for repetition, then, when you find it, decide which formulation was better and delete the other. Say you had written:

> It was a dreadful time for the company, a time of purest humiliation.

This would read much better using just the more specific of the two similar descriptions:

> It was a time of purest humiliation for the company.

That saves three words and strengthens the writing.

Cut as many adjectives and adverbs from your text as possible. Mark Twain famously said 'If you catch an adjective, Kill it!' The worse offenders are 'very' and 'quite'. If something is very big, it is large, if it is very, very big it is enormous. If it is quite small it is tiny. If you use the right word you don't need to qualify it with adjectives. Change

X was a strong business leader who was very resourceful

and replace it with:

X was a resourceful business leader.

You saved four words, and the text reads more precisely. X's strength is implied in his resourcefulness, so why use both adjectives?

You need to go through each paragraph individually and ask yourself 'What was I really trying to say?', 'Is this the best way to say it?' and 'Am I repeating myself?'

Repeating a point slows the pace of the writing and encourages impatient readers to start skipping chunks of text. Once that happens, they might stop believing in your story.

Look closely at what you have written. Test each word and phrase for accuracy and indispensability. Watch out for superfluous flab of adjectives and adverbs and delete unnecessary repetition. By this point you should find you have hit your word count.

Lastly, you should check that all your references comply with the standards laid down by your university (in the case of Bradford School of Management, this is Harvard Referencing). When you have done that you are ready to think about layout.

LAYOUT

Your university will set out standards of presentation. These will lay down rules about obligatory declaration pages, fonts, line spacing and margin size.

Create a word-processor template which applies these standards to all your text and then look at each page layout in turn.

1. Make sure your quotations are indented correctly and in the correct font.
2. Check that each new chapter opens on a new page.

3. Get rid of 'widows and orphans'. (A widow is the last line of a paragraph appearing at the top of a page, sundered from the rest, which is left behind on the previous page; an orphan is a heading or first line of a paragraph sitting at the bottom of a page, with the following text on the next one.) When you find one, insert a line of white space or a page break at a suitable point nearby, or cut or lengthen the text a little, so that the page break either falls between paragraphs or leaves at least two lines of a paragraph on each page. Work from the front of the file to the back, because removing one widow or orphan may create new ones further on. If your word processor has 'widow/orphan control' in its paragraph formatting options you can use this, but always do a final visual check, because automatic detection can occasionally produce strange layout results.

4. Make sure your captions are on the same page as your illustrations and that any surrounding text is appropriate.

5. Make sure your Table of Contents and Table of Illustrations are accurate.

If you have to submit a paper-bound copy, for marking or for your own use, make sure that the page set you send off for binding consists of a single, well-aligned, clearly printed copy of each page, all in the correct order and all the right way up.

None of these copy-editing and layout tasks are difficult, but they do take time and cannot be rushed. It is important to allow yourself plenty of time to carry out these mechanical processes at the end of dissertation-writing. If the dissertation is well presented the examiner approaches it with the thought that the student has taken care over detail, and so may well have taken care in research. If you complement good layout with clear, well-researched writing, then you have done everything you can to achieve a good result.

Enjoy your research, be polite to your reader, tell a good story and take pleasure in practising the craft of writing.

I wish you success with your dissertation, and your future career, and hope this little book has helped you on the way.

FURTHER READING

Chapter 1

Aristotle, translated Smith, Walter, & Gibson, Alan (2008) *Translations from the Organon of Aristotle*, BiblioBazaar, Charleston SC.

DeGroot, Gerard (2004) *The Bomb: A life*, Jonathan Cape, London.

Hughes, Jeff (2002) *The Manhattan Project: Big science and the atom bomb*, Icon Books, London.

Penrose, Roger (2004) *The Road to Reality*, Jonathan Cape, London.

Plato, translated Cornford, F.M. (1997) *Plato's Cosmology: 'Timaeus' of Plato*, Hackett Publishing, New York.

Zimmerman, David (1996) *Top Secret Exchange: The Tizard mission and the scientific war*, McGill-Queen's University Press, Montreal.

Chapter 2

Darwin, Charles (1998) [1859] *The Origin of Species*, Wordsworth Editions, London.

Gould, Stephen Jay (1986) 'Evolution and the triumph of homology, or why history matters', *American Scientist*, Jan.–Feb., pp. 60–69.

Hooke, Robert (2007) [1665] *Micrographia*, BiblioBazaar, Charleston SC.

Krause, Donald G. (1996) *Sun Tsu: The art of war for executives*, Nicholas Brealey, London.

Lomas, Robert (2009) *The Invisible College*, Transworld, London.

Wilmut, Ian, Campbell, Keith, & Tudge, Colin (2000) *The Second Creation: Dolly and the age of biological control*, Headline, London.

Wilson, Edward O. (1998) *Consilience: The unity of knowledge*, Knopf, New York.

Chapter 7

Aristotle, *see* http://classics.mit.edu/Aristotle/poetics.1.1.html (consulted July 2010).

Booker, Christopher (2004) *The Seven Basic Plots: Why we tell stories*, Continuum, London.

Dawkins, Richard (2006) *The God Delusion*, Bantam Press, London.

Dutton, Denis (2005) 'Are there seven basic plots?', *Washington Post*, 'Book World', 8 May.

Feynman, Richard (2007) *The Pleasure of Finding Things Out*, Penguin, London.

Kaku, Michio (2004) *Einstein's Cosmos*, Weidenfeld & Nicolson, London.

Lomas, Robert (2005) *Turning the Hiram Key*, Fair Winds Press, Rockport MA.

Pinker, Steven (1994) *The Language Instinct*, Penguin, London.

INDEX